PLONK
BUYER'S
GUIDE

David Biggs

Struik Publishers (Pty) Ltd
(a member of the Struik Publishing Group (Pty) Ltd)
Cornelis Struik House
80 McKenzie Street
Cape Town
8001

Reg. No.: 54/00965/07

First published in 1990, Faircape Books
2nd edition 1991
3rd edition 1992
4th edition 1993, Struik Publishers (Pty) Ltd
5th edition 1994
6th edition 1995
© David Biggs 1995

All rights reserved. No part of this publication may be reproduced, stored in a retrieval system, or transmitted, in any form or by any means, electronic, mechanical, by photocopying, recording or otherwise, without the prior written permission of the copyright owner.

Editors Richard Pooler and Sanette van der Mescht
DTP Design Mandy Moss

Reproduction by Hirt & Carter (Pty) Ltd, Cape Town
Printed and bound by CTP Book Printers, Parow

ISBN 1 86825 887 4

CONTENTS

The Wines on Our List *4*

Rating Plonk *5*

Biggs' Top 20 *6*

Don't Keep it Bottled Up *7*

Wine by Rail *8*

Learn the Language *9*

Dop for the Desperate *10*

The Best Wine in the World *11*

Home Improvements *13*

The Wines *14*

THE WINES ON OUR LIST

The South African Plonk Buyer's Guide 1996 is certainly not an exhaustive list of all the plonk produced in South Africa. To do that would be an impossible task, simply because we all have our own ideas about what is plonk and what isn't. This is simply a collection of wines designed for everyday drinking and sold at affordable (to most of us) prices.

This year we have decided to abandon the idea of setting a price limit to the wines. Prices fluctuate from store to store anyway, and many of the wines will have increased in price before the end of the year.

In the previous edition we tried to keep to below R8 a bottle. This year we've tried to keep to below R10, which is still a reasonable sum to pay for a bottle of liquid sunshine. Some of the wines listed are excellent value for money while others are reasonably pleasant or merely inoffensive. Then there are those which should just be avoided.

Remember too, that the ratings and opinions expressed here are very personal. You may not agree with all of them. Indeed, it would be very strange if you did, because wine is a personal thing. If everybody liked the same wines, there wouldn't be such a wide selection on the market.

Above all, don't take this book, or the wines it describes, seriously.

Wine is not a serious subject.

Wine is for fun.

So pull out a cork, fill your glass, relax and enjoy!

RATING PLONK

Bearing in mind that one man's wine is another man's wee-wee, to coin a nasty phrase, we hasten to say that our system of rating wines is very arbitrary and entirely personal. You may love some of the wines that have been awarded one miserable glass, and hate some of our top-rated ones. If this offends you, you're welcome to write to the author and tell him he's an ass.

To give readers a rough idea of what to expect from a wine, each one has been graded according to the 'three-glass rating system'. In any case, taste is a very personal thing and if you find a wine you like, at a price you can afford, go for it! Why worry whether the author likes it?

♉♉♉
If we've found the wine tasty and easy to drink in considerable quantities, it's probably been given a rating of three glasses. On the other hand, it may have been awarded three glass status simply because the taster had by that stage, reached the happy point when everything tastes good!

♉♉
Wines that are good, regular plonk for everyday drinking, without causing too much trauma, rate two glasses. Most plonks fall into this category. What do you expect at this sort of price?

♉
The one-star wines are all right in an emergency, but repeating the experience is not recommended. Still, it would be an awful waste to throw it away, so we have included a section on DIY wine improvement for those who can't bear to part with it after paying for it. Who knows, you may even make the stuff drinkable. If that seems like too much effort, chuck it out and get something else.

BIGGS'S TOP 20

As a wine writer I am often asked, "But what is your own, personal, favourite wine?" in the hope that I will reveal the name of the perfect wine. There simply isn't a 'best' wine. This means we can keep tasting and enjoying forever. If we discovered the 'perfect' wine, we'd stop tasting the others.

Different occasions call for different wines. There are heady, sweet fortified wines that are perfect for chilly evenings in front of a log fire. There are steely dry white wines to drink on a summer afternoon in the shade of a spreading vine, and there are fat, fruity dry reds to enjoy in good company, with a braai or a pizza.

I have pleasure in offering readers a list of 20 wines that have given me particular pleasure. Some are excellent wines, while others simply bring back delightful memories.

Backsberg Dry Red
This is always good value.

Blaauwklippen Social Dry Red
A lovely everyday red.

Delheim Pinotage Rosé
It now has a cheeky new label. Better than ever.

Eclipse Vivaldi
As good as wines costing three times the price!

Taverna Rouge
Some claim it's even nicer than Tassies!

Du Toitskloof Red Jerepigo
It warmed me on a long motorbike trip.

Lievland Lievlander
Consistently good.

Swartland Stein
Easy, off-dry white for any time.

Sedgewicks' Old Brown Sherry
Saves lives on a chilly canoe trip.

Lanzerac Rosé
It's been a favourite for many years.

Fairview Gamay Noir
A special drink for just once a year.

Windmeul Pinotage
I can't believe this price! Get some.

Montagu Mont Blanc
Off-dry, but with that Muscat nose. Magic!

Mamreweg Cinsaut
The plonk that inspired *The Plonk Buyer's Guide*.

Rooiberg Blanc Fumé Sur Lie
Terribly classy for the price!

Tassenberg
Everybody's first red wine. Bottled nostalgia.

Woolworths Dry Red (Tetrapak)
The most convenient wine package for a boat locker! Pleasant wine, too.

Valley Kaapse Keur
Off-dry and a nice touch of Hanepoot.

Vaughan Johnson's Seriously Good Plonk
Wonderful to have somebody who ADMITS to selling plonk!

Vredendal Fernao Pires
A spicy white wine with a difference.

DON'T KEEP IT BOTTLED UP!

If you want to hear strong language, ask almost any wine producer about the bureaucrats who run the wine industry. Mind you, bureaucrats aren't too popular in any industry. Luckily winemakers are a gutsy lot, and there have been head-on clashes with the authorities from time to time. So far the winemakers have scored some remarkable successes.

One of the silly regulations governing the South African wine industry is that certified wines must be sold only in regulation size glass bottles.

In other words, if you call a wine by the grape cultivar – Cabernet Sauvignon or Chardonnay, for example – you may not sell it in a plastic bottle or a bag-in-a-box. The same applies to any wine that has a vintage. You'll never see a box of 1994 Tassenberg. It would have to be sold in a bottle – that's why Tassies doesn't have vintages. It also can't be a wine of origin – Robertson, Stellenbosch, or Paarl, for example – if it is going into a box. The trouble is that glass bottles, with their imported corks and capsules, printed labels, protective cardboard sleeves and cartons, are about the most expensive form of packaging that's available. In many cases, about half the total cost of a case of wine goes in the packaging. It's far, far cheaper to pack wines in boxes or plastic bottles, or tetrapaks.

The bureaucrats say this would harm the 'image' of wine. Phooey! They're encouraging snobbery.

The good news is that several producers, like the Robertson Co-op, are putting a lot of pressure on the law makers to allow them to market good wines in their cheaper packaging.

When they win (and I'm sure they will), it will be a great day for us plonk drinkers. I, for one, will lop off the corner of a box of Cabernet and celebrate enthusiastically.

Sure there's a specially luxurious feeling about slicing off a lead capsule, drawing the cork with a good corkscrew and hearing that satisfying little 'plop'. But for those of us who simply like to drink the stuff as cheaply as possible, it's a big price to pay for a small plop.

WINE BY RAIL

Many South African wine drinkers have discovered the delights of mail order wine buying. It's an easy and very economical way of keeping your cellar well stocked with good wines.

Most wine cellars are happy to rail cases to their customers anywhere in the country. All you have to do is write to the cellar (or telephone them) and ask for their price list. This will be posted to you along with an order form and ordering instructions. Then you just send in your order and cheque (although some cellars include space for your credit card number, making payment even easier) and the wine will be on its way to you. Many cellars also include the latest railage tariffs, so you can work out what this will cost and add it to the total. It's useful to remember that a case of wine weighs about 17 kg.

Wine cellars have their lists of regular customers and send out new price lists whenever there are changes, so once you are on the mailing list, you will be kept up to date. Co-operative wineries, in particular, do a large proportion of their business by mail order, so they're well geared to handle your orders efficiently and despatch the wines to you without delay.

LEARN THE LANGUAGE

Wine snobs live in a different world. They certainly speak a different language. In this respect they're rather like lawyers and estate agents, who also have developed languages to disguise, rather than to reveal, what they're actually saying. The whole point of a special language is that you can make it so vague that it can mean anything you want it to, and later, if you should find your opinions differ from those of the 'experts', you can say, "Yes, that's exactly what I was saying all along".

In case you aspire to the higher regions of wine society (heaven forbid!), here are some common wine phrases in regular use, and some handy translations.

A rather organic nose – Stinks like compost.
Some nice firm tannins in this – My mouth feels like an inside out scrotum.
It has a lot of body – It has a lot of alcohol. I like it!
It needs a bit of time – It's totally undrinkable, but the winemaker is a sensitive chap and I'd hate to hurt his feelings.
An interesting wine – Sies! A urine sample is 'interesting' to a pathologist, but he doesn't have to DRINK the stuff! Alternatively, 'an interesting wine' often means, "I can't think of anything intelligent to say about this wine."
It has plenty of fruit – So what did you expect? Pork?
A lingering farewell – I'm not leaving while there's still some left in the bottle.
Noble rot – Yes, just listen to me.
Well balanced – Two bottles and I can still stand up.
It's a little tart – Tart? It's a real bitch if you ask me!
Very understated – Tasteless, bland, boring.
A lovely bouquet – I could drink a vase of it.
An unpretentious little wine – This stuff all tastes like Tassies to me.
A great nose and plenty of body – Who? Barbara Streisand?
It's a good food wine – If they don't serve snacks soon, I'm going to fall down.
Grassy – Maybe we should chuck it out on the lawn!
Great complexity – I'm using big words like 'complexity' to show that I'm still completely shober. Sorry, sober.
A very clean finish – Look, I haven't left a drop.
A very lively mousse – Has a kick like a lively mule.
A mellow wine – At this stage I'm everybody's good old pal.
Plenty of skin contact – This stuff is making me randy.

DOP FOR THE DESPERATE

There are wines for all sorts of drinkers, from the elegant, dignified and toffee-nosed to the dishevelled and downright drunk.

We plonk drinkers may believe we're down at the bottom end of the wine ladder with our Tassies, Virginia and Golden Alabama, but there are quite a few rungs below us. Frankly, we don't need to step on them, but it's interesting to know about them, and who knows, one day we may descend.

It all goes back to the days of the dreadful 'dop' system, when wine farmers paid their labourers partly in wine. The general idea was to keep the labourers in such a fuzzy mental state that they didn't realise they were being exploited and paid a pittance. And the wine with which they were paid was the dregs. Literally.

Today the 'dop' system has all but disappeared, and if wine farmers do supply their staff with wine, it is generally of a reasonable quality and usually in addition to a reasonable wage.

But many of the wine co-ops produce cheap wines, known locally as 'volkwyne' (wine for the people), which are never mentioned in the advertisements or displayed on the front shelves of the liquor stores.

A basic minimum wine price is laid down each year by the KWV, so the only way producers can cut the price to the bone, is by using cheaper and cheaper packaging. Conventional packaging – bottle, cork, label, carton, sleeve etc – costs more than a rand before a drop of wine goes into the bottle.

It's sometimes quite difficult to get information about these bottom-of-the-line wines, because the producers are not too proud of them, and there are always a lot of do-gooders who claim these volkwyne are ruining the downtrodden poor.

But if you're a volkwyn drinker, you'll know where to go for your supply. Downtrodden? Not with a kannetjie slung over the shoulder and a warm Saturday night ahead!

Often the wines are sold in bulk, and customers bring their own containers – anything from an empty paint can to a plastic bleach bottle will do.

Sometimes the wine is ready packed in what are known as 'papsakke' (floppy sacks), which are plastic sachets rather like those sometimes used for milk. The drinker simply bites off a corner and sucks away at the contents. If you haven't experienced one of these volkwyne, you're probably lucky. But hang around a country bottle store on a Saturday morning, and you'll see the customers for whom these cheap sub-plonks are what makes the weekend worthwhile.

Here's a roundup of some of these volkwyne. There are many more. They haven't been allocated ratings. Their customers couldn't care less what you or I may think of them.

Koes-Koes; Meaning 'duck-duck', the name refers to the fact that the buyer usually has to duck and dive on his way home from the bottle store so that his friends don't spot that he has a can of wine, or they'll probably try to cadge some from him.

Kanne vir die Manne; 'Cans for the men'. I suppose the idea behind this name is that you have to be a real man to withstand the kick of this powerful brew.

Hop, Johanna; I think this one's name came from the song, 'You give me Hope, Johanna'. Wherever it came from, it certainly gets its fans hopping.

Disco Stein; Another merry musical wine for a Saturday party.

Skelmpie; 'Sneaky little one' Probably appropriately named. These wines do tend to sneak up on one.

Rooikat; 'It will have you yowling at the moon like a cat on heat,' they say.

So there you are. That's what they're drinking at the bottom of the wine ladder. Cheers to them all!

THE BEST WINE IN THE WORLD

Wine is for fun. Anybody who drinks it for any other reason is a fool.

Yet there are those who feel they must drink dry red wine because it is fashionable, or who shun semi-sweet wines because they feel their neighbours might consider them unsophisticated.

And there are always the wine snobs who care only about the rarity and expense of the wine they serve, in order to impress their guests. For them an imported wine will always be considered better than a home-grown one.

Fools, all of them!

The plonk drinker doesn't really care what somebody else paid for a wine, as long as it tastes good.

He or she certainly cares what they paid for the wine they bought themselves, because they want to get the most fun for their money.

Wine is the stuff which bonds friends together. A bottle drunk alone is a wasted bottle. Wine should be shared with friends, flavoured with good conversation and spiced with kind humour.

Think of the truly memorable bottles of wine you've enjoyed and the chances are you won't even remember the label. You'll remember the friends who shared it with you and the occasion on which you opened the bottle.

My own great wine memories include the opening of a bottle of warming Old Brown Sherry in a canoe on the Breede River with a group of fellow paddlers, all freezing after a very wet descent down some rapids.

And I remember the warmth we derived from drinking cheap Uruguayan wine in the cosy cabin of a yacht, far in the south Atlantic, as the sun set over an icy sea. It all made the hardship of the voyage seem worthwhile.

I'll never forget a farewell drink of very cheap wine on Signal Hill, when a good friend left the newspaper world to start his own business. We, his colleagues, couldn't have chosen a more appropriate libation to send him on his way with our best wishes. I don't have any idea what wine it was, but it came from a five litre jar, passed from hand to hand around the circle: nectar.

So, leave the snobbery to those whose lives are empty of real friends and whose sense of fun has been shrivelled by a mean and grasping lifestyle.

Plonk drinkers know the very best wine in the world. It's the one you share with friends.

HOME IMPROVEMENTS

No, we're not talking fitting shelves or adding a granny flat here. This is about improving a bad wine once you've got it home.

Every so often you do get a box or bottle of wine that is frankly just too dreadful to drink.

This raises a painful problem for the true plonk devotee. Drink it and your teeth will probably rot. Throw it away and a) you'll have wasted the money and b) you'll be left with nothing to drink all evening.

So let's see whether we can improve on the wine. A good wine first aid kit always includes a bottle of sweet hanepoot and one of cheap port.

Cheap red wines that are dreadful are usually raw and tannic. One sip and the inside of your mouth wrinkles up like a silk shirt that's been slept in.

The answer is to sweeten things by adding a good dollop of sweet port. This should make things bearable. If it doesn't help, try turning the whole lot into a warming Gluwein. Put the wine into a pot, add a cup of brown sugar, a few slices of lemon, a grating of nutmeg and a powdering of cinnamon and warm it all up on the stove, stirring regularly.

Well, it's better that chucking it all away, isn't it?

White wine that's too bad even for a plonk drinker is probably too acid. You can almost feel the enamel peeling from you teeth as you sip it.

Add instant sweetness with a healthy splash of fortified Hanepoot Jerepigo. White Muscadel will do at a pinch, but it's a shame to waste it in an experiment that may not work. Muscadel is rather classy stuff.

If none of these ideas help to make the wine palatable, it wasn't worth drinking anyway, so all you've lost is a little *soetes*. Just make sure you've kept enough hanepoot or port to use as a consolation if the experiment fails.

AAN DE DOORNS CO-OP
PO Box 235, Worcester 6849
Tel: (0231) 72301 * Fax: (0231) 74626

The Worcester cellar is situated near the Breede River on the new road to Villiersdorp and they're happy to send wine by rail. At Aan de Doorns a whole range of very drinkable wines are produced, most of them at modest prices. The wines are sold by the case or in packs of four bottles.

Blanc de Noir ♈♈
A pretty, very pale coral wine made from South Africa's own grape, Pinotage. Slightly 'cool-drinky' but pleasant if well chilled. A frivolous little party wine.

Clairette ♈♈
A dry white wine that's excellent value and consistently good, year after year. Fruity and drinkable for everyday quaffing.

Sauvignon Blanc ♈♈♈
Good value. An amazingly elegant little wine for its price. This will certainly impress your snobby friends.

Chardonnay ♈♈
Not bad to have a Chardonnay at a plonk price! Thinnish and very citrus-character, unwooded– well, at this price!

Colombar ♈♈
Made semi-sweet, a pleasant enough wine for casual drinking.

Laat Oes Steen ♈♈
A very fruity, juicy, semi-sweet wine made from Chenin Blanc. I'm told it's one of the cellar's best sellers.

Pinotage ♈♈
Good everyday drinking and cheaper than Tassies. Ideal for rugby watching.

Vin Rouge ♈♈♈
Now here's a wine for men! Made from Pinotage and Cinsaut, at 14 percent alcohol it has a kick like Joel Stransky. Roughish, too. Ideal for that after-match braai.

Ruby Cabernet 🍷🍷
It's interesting to find a Ruby Cabernet in this price range. Quite a pleasant, easy-drinking red wine. Thinnish, but with lots of alcohol.

Port 🍷🍷
Great to find a port that fits the plonk pattern. There's lots of raisiny sweetness in this one, but unlike most ports, it hasn't been matured in wood. Nice warming stuff, though.

AGTERKLIPHOOGTE CO-OP
PO Box 267, Robertson 6705
Tel: (02351) 61103 * Fax: (02351) 3329

This little cellar is off the beaten tourist track, but well worth a visit. Visits are by appointment only, so phone ahead. Most of the wines produced here go to the big wholesalers, but there are some bargains to be had at the cellar, even though the list is limited.

Colombard 🍷🍷🍷
An excellent example of what can be done with Colombard, which is made better in the Robertson area than anywhere else. A dry wine with a big guava aroma; nice clean flavour. Consistently good value.

Blanc de Blanc 🍷🍷
This is also made from Colombard grapes, but has a hint of sweetness. The acid balance gives it a nice crisp character. It's a good wine to have with food.

ASHTON CO-OP
PO Box 40, Ashton 6715
Tel: (0234) 51135 * Fax: (0234) 51284

This co-op will rail wines to you (you pay the railage) and charge them to your credit card. It's well worth phoning for a price list and order form. Excellent value for money wines can be found here.

Bukettraube 🍷🍷🍷
A fresh, light and fragrant white wine, full of honey flavours. The soft sweetness is nicely balanced by just the right amount of acidity. Try this with a good Malay Babotie! Perfect!

Colombar ♈♈♈
Really excellent value! The Robertson area has become known for its fine Colombard wines and when you've tasted this one you'll know exactly why. It's the sort of plonk you can drink happily all day and look forward to opening another bottle. It's worth buying this one by the case!

Dry Red ♈♈
Any wine that's honest enough to call itself 'Dry Red' gets my vote every time. This is a fine, straightforward and very drinkable, everyday red plonk. It needs no fancy description and the bottle is sealed with a screw cap. A blended wine to drink without any fuss.

Gewürztraminer ♈♈♈
An off-dry white wine with all the flavours and scents of a tropical fruit salad. Delicious for drinking on its own or with lightly spiced foods. Great value!

Late Harvest ♈♈
Semi-sweet and juicy, this is an uncomplicated, sunny wine to be enjoyed well chilled.

White Muscadel ♈♈♈
Here's the wine for the sweet of tooth. Full of raisin sweetness, but not heavy or cloying. This delicate and charming wine is a winner!

Red Muscadel ♈♈♈
A good, honey-sweet *soetes* at a sensible price! Full of raisiny charm and muscat aromas, this is a warming fortified drink to sip on a chilly evening.

Sauvignon Blanc ♈♈♈
An unusually soft and smooth Sauvignon Blanc, unwooded and very reasonably priced. Sauvignon Blancs are usually rather expensive, so this is great value. In fact, it would fit in well with a really up-market dinner.

Special Late Harvest ♈♈
A pleasant, slightly light-bodied semi-sweet white wine with an attractive, clean aftertaste. Lunch-time drinking.

Riesling ♈♈
A dry white wine at a very modest price. Light and smooth.

Weisser Riesling ♟♟♟
Made semi-sweet, this is a classy wine, packed with flavour and easy to drink. It's not hard to see why it regularly wins awards.

AUTUMN HARVEST WINES

Made by SFW and available from bottle stores everywhere.

Ausberger ♟♟
This off-dry white wine would be quite bland if it were not for a slight hint of muscat honey. Easy drinking.

Country Claret ♟♟
A light-bodied red wine, smooth and simple. Almost sweet.

Crackling ♟♟♟
In spite of its 'down-market' image, this is a splendid little wine. It even has a gold medal to its credit! Very popular in the Eastern Cape. It's a dry white wine with a gentle prickle of tiny bubbles on the tongue and plenty of fruitiness on the nose. It goes very well with fish or chicken and is available in several sizes. Serve chilled.

Grand Crû ♟♟
Very dry, but well-made wine. It's sold in five-litre boxes, making it a useful wine to have in the kitchen. Try using wine instead of vinegar for a change of cooking style. And you can sip while you simmer!

Late Vintage ♟♟
A nice, juicy, inexpensive semi-sweet white wine for everyday quaffing.

Stein ♟♟
Another semi-sweet, general purpose house wine. It is pleasant and easy drinking, particularly if well chilled. Makes a good spritzer with soda water on a hot summer's day.

AVONTUUR ESTATE
PO Box 1128, Somerset West 7129
Tel: (024) 553450 * Fax: (024) 554600

This attractive winery on the mountain slopes is well known for its thoroughbred horses, as well as its innovative wines. Winemaker Jean-Luc Sweerts is a charming Frenchman, with a very smooth line in chat. A nice place to visit. Good value wines, but only one really fits into our plonk category.

Blanc de Noir ♟♟
A pretty little wine made from Pinot Noir grapes. Off-dry and cheerful for a party. Very good when slightly chilled.

BACKSBERG ESTATE
PO Box 1, Klapmuts 7625
Tel: (02211) 5141 * Fax: (02211) 5144

Backsberg has been producing good, everyday wines at sensible prices for many years. Whether you regard them as 'plonk' is a matter of opinion. Their dry red wine certainly deserves a place in the plonk-lover's cellar.

Dry Red ♟♟♟
This reliable, everyday red wine is a real find. It remains one of the rare treasures waiting to be discovered by those who explore the Cape's wine routes. It has as much flavour and character as many wines costing twice the price. You could open a bottle for a very formal occasion without fear.

BADSBERG CO-OP
PO Box 72, Rawsonville 6845
Tel: (0231) 91120 * Fax: (0231) 91122

All the wines in the small range produced by this cellar are very modestly priced. And they're happy to rail wines to you anywhere (as long as you pay the railage). If you live too far away to visit, send them a fax and ask for a price-list. There's an order form attached.

Badlese ♟♟
Quite a fruity, semi-sweet white wine with just enough sweetness for those who like a bit of sugar. Easy drinking.

Riesling ♉♉
A crisp, light dry white wine with some sweet, grassy aroma. Pleasant and refreshing, it goes well with food. Serve chilled.

Laat Oes ♉♉
A semi-sweet white wine which is full of ripe and fruity flavour.

Blanc de Blanc ♉♉♉
An unusual plonk this. Full of character. Blended from Chardonnay, Riesling and Colombard. Almost dry, but with a small amount of fruity sweetness for interest. Good value!

Vin Sec ♉♉
This is something rather unusual for the Plonk Guide. A Sparkling wine at plonk price! Badsberg's Vin Sec is a pleasant, carbonated bubbly, slightly sweetish, but quite clean and fresh. I think it would make an ideal mix with orange juice at a Champagne breakfast.

BARRYDALE CO-OP
PO Box 59, Barrydale 6750
Tel: (028) 5721012 * Fax: (028) 5721541

This Little Karoo winery makes some really splendid wines, but in small quantities, so they are often sold out early in the year. It's worth getting their latest price list and ordering a few cases.

Blanc de Noir ♉♉
A very pale pink wine with a heady scent of Muscadel, but it's less sweet than the nose leads you to expect. Nicely balanced and very pleasant. It's a good lunch-time wine, as the alcohol content is quite low.

Droë Rooi ♉♉♉
An honest, easy-drinking, dry red wine with no pretensions to greatness. Based on Cinsaut, which is the grape that made Tassies famous, but this blend also contains some aristocrats, like Merlot.

BEAUFORT WINES

Sold in five-litre boxes, this is a house brand of the Solly Kramer's group of liquor stores. Reliable, good, everyday plonks at modest prices. Good value.

Blanc de Blanc ♈♈
A rather lightweight, but easy-quaffing white wine.

Blanc de Noir ♈♈
A pale-pink wine, semi-sweet and fruity. Slightly cloying on the palate, but good if served chilled.

Dry Red ♈♈
This is a fruity, easy-drinking, unpretentious red wine you can drink at any time.

Stein ♈♈
Semi-sweet and possibly a bit sticky for some palates. Might go rather well with Chinese takeaways.

BLAAUWKLIPPEN
PO Box 54, Stellenbosch 7599
Tel: (021) 8800133 * Fax: (021) 8801250

Blaauwklippen is one of the more up-market wine cellars that now produces good, everyday plonks at reasonable prices, as well as their more famous wines. Let's hope other cellars follow suit soon.

Sociable Dry Red ♈♈♈
What a charming name for a relaxed, easy-drinking red wine. A nice, low acidity makes it a smooth wine, pleasantly plummy and soft on the palate. Just what every plonk drinker looks for.

Sociable White ♈♈
This is a soft, easy-drinking off-dry white wine designed to be enjoyed young and fresh. The low alcohol makes it an ideal lunch-time wine.

BUYERS' OWN BRAND (BOB)

These budget-priced wines are available at stores in the Drop Inn and Aroma group. They are well worth trying.

BOB Blanc de Blanc ♈♈
A relaxed, comfortable wine from the Paarl district. Made mostly from Chenin Blanc.

BOB Chardonnay ♟♟♟
Almost too good to be classified as a plonk, this is a rare find. The wine is lightly wooded and has some fresh citrus scents blended with the warm butterscotch flavours.

BOB Blended Red ♟♟
Smooth and easy-drinking, made from Cabernet and Tinta Barocca from the Malmesbury area. Rather a comfortable, slippers-and-pipe sort of wine.

BOLAND WYNKELDER
PO Box 2, Huguenot 7645
Tel: (02211) 626190\1 * Fax: (02211) 625379

Some excellent plonks are produced here and the handy little 500ml Bon Vino dumpie bottles are ideal for picnics or storing on board your boat. Bon Vino also comes in five-litre boxes. They're good value. Boland Co-op will rail wines to you anywhere in the country. These obliging folk will even rail mixed cases to you.

Chenin Blanc ♟♟♟
Some very tantalising fruit salad aromas help to make this an attractive dry white wine. Fresh and juicy, best enjoyed young.

Late Harvest ♟♟
A very soft, semi-sweet white wine with a scent of honey. Easy-drinking.

Pinotage ♟♟
Pretty good value, this. A Pinotage with a little wood maturation, selling for less than ten rands from the cellar.

Bon Vino Dry ♟♟
A delicate white wine with a crisp, clean character for summer drinking, served chilled. Available from the winery only.

Bon Vino Semi-sweet ♟♟
Made from Chenin Blanc and full of nice fruity flavour. Easy drinking and sold only at the Co-op.

Bon Vino Red ♟♟
An ideal, light-bodied red wine to take on a picnic or boat. Easy drinking and undemanding. Good value.

Hanepoot Jerepiko ♟♟
No plonk-drinker's wine store is complete without a good, rich Hanepoot Jerepiko. This one has the honey nose and ripe, sunny flavour that keeps Hanepoot at the top of the plonker's pops.

Bukettraube ♟♟
A wonderfully spicy off-dry wine with plenty of fruity character and a nice clean finish. An elegant plonk.

Late Harvest ♟♟
A semi-sweet white wine with a subtle honey-laden nose and full fruity flavour. Very reasonably priced.

BONNIEVALE CO-OP
PO Box 206, Bonnievale 6730
Tel: (02346) 2795 * Fax: (02346) 2332

This attractive little cellar, two kilometres outside the picturesque town of Bonnievale, is well worth a visit if you're in the area. They produce a very good 500ml dumpie bottled range of everyday plonks called Kelkiewyn.

Blanc de Blanc ♟♟
A pleasantly clean, dry white wine for summer drinking. Serve nicely chilled for a real treat.

Colombar ♟♟
Made just off-dry, this is typical of the Colombards of this area, with delicate guava aroma and rather a pleasant, easy-drinking fruity character.

Pinotage ♟♟
A smooth and light-bodied claret-type red wine, easy to drink with no pretensions. It's light enough to serve slightly chilled on a warm day.

BOPLAAS ESTATE
PO Box 156, Calitzdorp 6660
Tel: (04437) 33326 * Fax: (04437) 33750

Boplaas is probably best known for its fine port, but Carel Nel makes a wide range of good wines, two of which could be classed as plonk, although the maker might be a little hurt by the title.

Blanc de Noir ♉♉♉
Pretty orange-pink colour with wafts of flowery scents and a slightly sweet flavour. Nice, crisp finish from just the right degree of acidity. A delicious wine.

Dry Red ♉♉♉
Packed with complex fruity flavours, this is a great summer wine with quite a low alcohol content. Superb flavour, with hints of strawberry.

BOTHA CO-OP
PO Botha, 6857
Tel and Fax: (02324) 740

This small co-op on the Breede River produces some excellent red and white wines in very limited quantities for sale from the co-op. Some of them fall within our plonk price range and are well worth buying.

Blanc de Noir ♉♉
A fruity, pale-pink light-bodied wine with some Cabernet scents. Good for casual quaffing. Try this with pork chops.

Cabernet Sauvignon ♉♉♉
I've heard experienced wine lovers claim that this is the best value budget Cabernet on the market. It has been given some oak maturation, and still manages to retain a low price. Made for early drinking, but could easily last a year or two.

Chardonnay ♉♉
A very light, easy-drinking Chardonnay at a reasonable price. Not the usual heavy, South African style, but certainly not boring.

Chenin Blanc ♉♉
This off-dry wine is full of juicy fruitiness and has quite a pleasant acid balance.

Chenin Blanc Late Harvest 🍷🍷
It's nice to have two similar wines with different degrees of sweetness. If you like something on the sweet side, you'll probably enjoy this. Nice and juicy, but not sticky.

Merlot 🍷🍷
Probably one of the most trendy wine cultivars around these days. It's worth buying this just to impress your snob friends and show that you appreciate a good Merlot. What's more, it tastes good. Not too complicated, and very easy to drink.

Riesling 🍷
Rather an ordinary dry white wine.

Sauvignon Blanc 🍷🍷🍷
A very satisfying white wine, with lots of exciting flavour, at a price you shouldn't miss. Actually, this is a very respectable wine and would probably be insulted to be called plonk.

Weisser Riesling 🍷🍷
A very pleasant little wine, made just off-dry to add interest. A rather good everyday plonk and the perfect companion to bobotie.

BOTTELARY CO-OP
PO Box 16, Koelenhof 7605
Tel: (021) 8822204 * Fax: (021) 8822205

Tucked away at the back of Stellenbosch's Papegaaiberg, this co-op is well worth a visit. Their bright labels depicting South African birds are very eye-catching. Bottelary will rail case-lots to customers and charge them to your credit card.

Adelrood 🍷🍷
A reliable, everyday dry red with a slightly smoky character and some jammy fruitiness, but enough tannin to give it a robust bite.

Blanc de Noir 🍷🍷
An off-dry wine with a pretty, golden peach colour. Nice spicy scent and easy, relaxed flavour for casual drinking. Serve cold.

Pinotage 🍷🍷🍷
A really nice, smooth red wine. Unwooded and low in tannin. An honest, everyday drinking plonk which usually sells out early in the season.

Special Late Harvest ♆♆♆
Quite a delicate wine, with nice fruit-salad flavours. Not as sweet as most Special Late Harvests. Low alcohol makes it ideal for midday quaffing.

BOVLEI CO-OP
PO Box 82, Wellington 7655
Tel: (02211) 31567 * Fax: (02211) 31386

The quality of Bovlei's wines has improved in recent years. Their red wines have risen out of the plonk category, but some of the whites are still priced comfortably within our range. They're happy to rail wines and charge them to your card.

Stein ♆♆
A semi-sweet white wine for everyday drinking. Pleasant guava scents and a nice fruity character.

Bukettraube ♆♆
This semi-sweet white wine has a delightful honey muscat scent and a very juicy, fruit salad flavour.

Grand Cru ♆♆
A very steely-dry white wine. Rather austere for some of us, but very clean and crisp.

Red Hanepoot ♆♆
We all know that Hanepoot is white, so the mere fact of having a red Hanepoot makes it a conversation piece. It's sweet and raisiny and lots of fun. A light sweet wine for easy summer drinking.

Wellington Dry Red (dumpies) ♆♆
A very practical red plonk in a convenient six-pack for picnics and parties. Wonderful value.

Wellington Dry White (dumpies) ♆♆
Clean and fresh, an uncomplicated dry white wine for any old time.

Wellington Semi-Sweet (dumpies) ♆♆
The ideal spritzer wine in a handy six-pack. Cheerful and fruity. Good value.

Tapsak ♆
You get four wines in this floppy-pack range. There's a semi-sweet white, dry white, red and rose. They come in a five-litre plastic bag with a tap at the bottom. A bit clumsy to handle, but very cheap and cheerful. Quite drinkable.

BRANDVLEI CO-OP
PO Box 595, Worcester 6849
Tel and Fax: (0231) 94215

A remarkable winery where the price list hasn't changed for some years and almost everything costs about R5 a bottle.

Cinsaut ♈♈♈
Cinsaut is one of South Africa's really 'honest' red wines. It's fruity and light and easy to drink. No wonder it is used to make our most famous plonks, like Tassies. And this one costs about the same as Tassies. The plonk lover's dream!

Blanc de Noir ♈♈
A nice, peachy coloured semi-sweet wine. Fruity and juicy. Nice served chilled. Good value.

Chardonnay ♈♈
Good grief! A chardonnay for five rand! Unbelievable! Go for it! You can't go wrong. At this price you can even use it for cooking.

Riesling ♈♈
Just because it's cheap, don't take it lightly. It won a gold medal at the Veritas competition. Not stunning, but Cape Rieslings are not noted for their complexity. Easy, dry and crisp. Ideal for casual quaffing.

Sauvignon Blanc ♈♈
Dry and crisp at an amazing price. Great value for this noble cultivar. It is made for easy, relaxed drinking, but is elegant enough with a great meal.

Petillant Xandre ♈♈
Here's an interesting one. Just a hint of bubbles, and a fruity, semi-sweet flavour. Nice for a party.

Port ♈♈
What a pleasure to find a port at this plonk price! Great for the end of a good meal, or just for drinking on a cold day. It may not match up to the expensive stuff, but it's rich and warming.

Hanepoot Jerepiko ♈♈♈
Now here's a plonk lover's treasure! Rich and sweet, full of honey flavour and at a price you can afford. Keep a bottle handy to soften anything you buy that's too acid. Splash a little over ice-cream for a wonderful dessert.

CALITZDORP CO-OP
PO Box 193, Calitzdorp 6660
Tel: (04437) 33301 Fax: (04437) 33110

Calitzdorp is fast becoming known as the port capital of South Africa. This co-op produces some fine ports at quite modest prices. Their table wines are not bad either. They rail wines to all provinces – see their price list. Very useful.

Blanc de Noir
A winner in its class at the Klein Karoo show, so you should be impressed. A delicious semi-sweet wine with a pale golden orange colour and pleasantly low acidity, which makes it smooth and quaffable. Delicious for a summer lunch.

Pinotage
A smooth, soft and uncomplicated red wine with some nice rich berry flavours, for easy, everyday enjoyment. Unwooded and unpretentious.

Red Muscadel
What a pleasure to get a good *soetes* in the plonk price range! Lovely spicy flavours, typical of the Karoo veld. Warm and satisfying to keep out the chill on a frosty night.

White Muscadel
Very similar to the Red Muscadel, apart from the colour. A super wine for those with a sweet tooth.

Cabernet
Cabernet usually costs much more than this. It's even been matured in oak barrels for a few months. Definitely a super-plonk. Great value.

Ruby Port
A mouth-filling, juicy port to end a good meal, or simply to sip on a chilly evening.

Full Cream Sherry
It's unusual to find sherry at a plonk price, but this sweetish one is proving popular.

Capenheimer
This unusual wine is made by Monis of Paarl and sold in liquor stores everywhere. It's a light, semi-sweet white wine with a tiny bubble. Not popular among wine snobs, but plonk lovers know it's full of flavour and lightness. The ideal wine to drink chilled on a hot day.

CAPE STYLE WINES

Safe and middle-of-the-road, these everyday plonks are sold at very reasonable prices.

Late Harvest ♟♟
A semi-sweet white with no pretensions. Might make a good spritzer.

Stein ♟♟
Semi-sweet, but quite fruity. A relaxed little wine.

Dry Red ♟♟
Plain, wholesome drinking. Light-bodied and quite fruity.

Grand Crû ♟♟
Fine, if you like your wine arid. Crisp and clean.

Catalina ♟♟
You have to search quite hard to find this cheapie. It is available only in one or two selected Stellenbosch bottle stores. It's made by one of the better-known Stellenbosch estates, whose winemaker threatened to scrag me if I revealed that he had perpetrated this wine. It's a great favourite with regular customers, who refer to it as *Rooi Rok*, because of the dress worn by the smiling girl on the label. Cheap and cheerful. Sold in a one-litre bottle with a screw-cap.

CEDERBERG KELDERS
PO Cederberg, 8136
Tel: (02682) 1531

The prices of most of the wines produced by this mountain cellar are slightly above our plonk limit. They are happy to supply buyers by mail order, so send for a price list!

Pinotage ♟♟
A nice, soft red wine for everyday drinking on its own or with food.

CELLAR CASK WINES

This is one of the oldest ranges of boxed wines in South Africa. They're made by Distillers Corporation in Stellenbosch and have earned a reputation for consistent quality. They're usually sold in five-litre boxes, but have appeared in several other guises.

Johannisberger Select Red ♈♈
A blended dry red wine, not spectacular, but good value and reliable. Keep a box in the kitchen.

Johannisberger Select White ♈♈♈
A semi-sweet white wine with some good ripe grape flavour and not too much harsh acidity. A nice summer wine when served well chilled. An acceptable everyday plonk.

CITRUSDAL CO-OP
PO Box 41, Citrusdal 7340
Tel: (022) 9212233 * Fax: (022) 9213937

In the heart of the wild flower area, this enterprising co-op has become known for its attractive wine labels, some of them decorated with specially commissioned flower paintings. The wines are sold under the Goue Vallei *label. They give a discount if you buy more than four cases.*

Blanc de Noir ♈♈
An attractive, pale pink wine with more than a touch of fruit. The perfect match for a bobotie. It's also ideal to sip while watching the cricket on television on a hot summer afternoon. Serve chilled.

Classique Rouge ♈♈♈
I think they put all the odd leftovers into this fine red plonk. It's very good. Lots of big, gutsy flavour to go with winter stews or a venison pie. A fine plonk at a good price.

Blanc de Blanc ♈♈
A juicy, off-dry white wine with a fruity bouquet.

Weisser Riesling ♈♈
A mouth-filling, semi-sweet wine with a very juicy, fruity character.

Late Vintage ♈♈
A reliable, but straight forward, semi-sweet white wine.

CLAIRVAUX CELLAR
PO Box 179 Robertson 6705
Tel: (02351) 3842 * Fax (02351) 61925

A pleasant and friendly cellar to visit. Try to get there at the end of the pressing season, when they hold a little street party, with all sorts of goodies made from must. They'll rail wines to you, and give you a 10 percent discount if you buy 10 or more cases.

Sauvignon Blanc ♟♟
A rather elegant and delicate dry wine. Crisp grassy character.

Rhine Riesling ♟♟
Wine with a slightly turpentine nose, which is typical of the varietal. An off-dry.

Rhine Riesling Late Harvest ♟♟
A semi-sweet white wine with a nice rich bouquet.

Hopp Johanna ♟♟
Hey, this is the wine to take home and impress your friends! A genuine people's plonk, it's described by the cellarmaster as a "smiling, sweet red wine". Very cheap for a fortified wine. It is available in a glass bottle for formal occasions, a plastic one for casual drinking (and you can drop it without damage) or a 500ml dumpie bottle for sissies. If you don't buy this one, you're not a devoted plonkoholic.

Somerkleur Late Harvest $
A semi-sweet white wine sold in a five-litre box at a very modest price.

Somerkleur Ruby Red ♟
An everyday red plonk in a box.

CULEMBORG WINES

These very reliable wines are unashamedly plonk, excellent value and without any unpleasant surprises. Interestingly enough, they've established quite a good export market in several overseas countries. They can't be too bad, hey!

Blanc de Noir ♟♟♟
A fruity, semi-sweet white wine that's easy to drink. It has a rather attractive peachy-pink colour. One of the best *Plonks de Noir* available.

Claret 🍷
A light-bodied red wine, made from Cinsaut and Pinotage. It has an almost sweetish flavour, but is soft and easy to drink.

Grand Crû 🍷
A clean, dry white wine with a nice acid tang to it. Easy-drinking and good value.

Late Harvest 🍷
A rather pleasant, sweetish white wine, with plenty of fruity character, but enough acidity to prevent it from being sticky. Good value.

Light 🍷
One of the very few low-alcohol wines with some flavour. OK, it's a bit thin, but it's better than most of the light ones.

Dancers 🍷
Available only in selected Stellenbosch bottle stores, not in the affluent parts of the town. Very cheap and cheerful and made by one of the Cape's most successful winemakers, who wishes to remain anonymous, for some inexplicable reason. It's sometimes referred to as 'Travolta' because of the dancers on the label. Not bad, really, but quite hard to find if you don't happen to live near the right store.

DE DOORNS CO-OP
PO Box 129, De Doorns 6875
Tel: (02322) 2835 * Fax: (02322) 2100

If you have the time, stop at this wonderful Karoo winery just off the N1. The prices are really low and there are real bargains to be found. The most expensive wine on their latest price list is just over R6 a bottle. Beat that! They're geared for mail-order business, so give them a call.

Roodehof 🍷
Here's a simple, easy-quaffing dry red wine at a very modest price. It's worth keeping a few bottles on hand for casual drinking at a braai or when you're watching rugby or... well, just about any time.

Blanc de Blanc 🍷
A rather pleasant, dry, blended white wine to drink with your take-away chicken.

Chenin Blanc ♀♀
A clean semi-sweet white wine, light-bodied and uncomplicated for everyday drinking.

Colombar ♀♀♀
Off-dry and with a touch of sunny, guava character. A really excellent wine to keep for drinking at any old time.

Late Vintage ♀♀
A typical semi-sweet plonk. Not remarkable, but safe and fruity. This will find plenty of followers.

Perlé Blanc ♀♀
A semi-sweet sparkling wine at a remarkably low price. Ideal for a birthday party and other celebrations. You can also mix it with orange juice for a champagne breakfast.

Premier Grand Crû ♀♀
Like the advertisement says, it's good and clean and fresh, tra-la-la, but not very exciting. Actually, not bad if you want a simple dry wine for every day.

Stein ♀♀
A simple semi-sweet wine. Serve well chilled.

Hanepoot ♀♀♀
Typical sweet Hanepoot, full of golden sunshine and honey. Just try this after a chilly kreef dive! It'll get the senses tingling.

Sherry ♀♀
This is a medium-sweet sherry, nice and warming and fine for the start of a party. A friendly drink. What a pity sherry isn't so popular any more.

COGMAN'S CO-OP Winery
PO Box 332, Montagu, 6720
Tel: (0234) 41340 * Fax: (0234) 42113.

This little Montagu co-op sells some well-priced plonks. When you're visiting the hot springs, take a day off and try some of these bargains. Their port was a champion in the Klein Karoo wine show.

Riesling ♀♀
An uncomplicated dry white wine for casual drinking. No great shakes, but reliable.

Sauvignon Blanc ♀♀♀
A very classy little wine, this! It was judged the best in its class and you can see why. Impress your snooty friends with it.

Colombard ♀♀♀
This very delicious wine is made off-dry, and that touch of sweetness is well balanced by the right degree of acidity.

Late Harvest ♀♀
A good, juicy semi-sweet wine at a plonk price.

Muscat de Alexandrie ♀♀
Now here's something a bit different! Hanepoot that's not completely sweet and sticky. This one has been made semi-sweet, and it has all the wonderful honey-muscat aroma you get with the fortified one, but not so much sweetness. Worth a try.

Red Muscadel ♀♀♀
A really splendid sweet wine, packed with sunshine and raisins. Chill it, pour it over crushed ice or sip it by the fireside. A year-round *soetes*.

Port ♀♀♀
Well, it's a champion in its region. And at this price it should be a champion in your wine cellar too. Good, warming stuff for winter.

DE HELDERBERG CO-OP
PO Box 71, Firgrove 7110
Tel: (024) 422370 * Fax: (024) 422373

Situated between Stellenbosch and Somerset West, this is a convenient co-op for Capetonians to visit. The wines have a reputation for consistently high quality and many of them are now being exported. A cheaper range of wines, under the Protea label, has been introduced for us plonk drinkers.

Blanc de Noir ♀♀
Quite a dark pink for a Blanc de Noir. I'd call it a Rosé, actually. Soft, semi-sweet, easy to drink.

Cabernet Sauvignon ♀♀♀
Remarkably good value. Quite a serious 'Cab', this. Lots of complex fruit and spiciness.

De Zoete Roodt ♉♉
A very unusual wine – a semi-sweet red. It's particularly delicious when served chilled. Nice juicy flavours and quite a low alcohol content.

Pinotage ♉♉
Quite a rich, big red wine. You could lay this one down for a year or two and you'd have a really superior wine!

Shiraz ♉♉
A rich, spicy red wine for plonk drinkers with big cupboards. Like the Pinotage, it will improve with age. But who ever heard of a plonk drinker with patience?

Vin Rouge ♉♉
An unpretentious, everyday red plonk with a loyal following. It's available in convenient 500 ml screw-cap dumpies at a very reasonable price.

DELHEIM WINES
PO Box 10, Koelenhof 7605
Tel: (021) 8822033 * Fax: (021) 8822036

Delheim produces one of my favourite pink plonks. Most of the wines produced at this very active cellar fall outside our price range. It's worth a visit, but preferably not at the height of the tourist season, when things become rather hectic. Always a cheerful bear-hug from ebullient vintner Spatz Sperling, who seems to have become used to being included in the plonk guide now, even though the idea appalled him at first.

Pinotage Rosé ♉♉♉
A very fresh, fruity pink wine with attractive wafts of strawberry scents and soft, sweetish flavours. It's light and easy to drink, with a clean finish. Ideal for South Africa's climate. There should be more wines like this. Serve chilled.

Roodewijn ♉♉
A blend of whatever's available, so it changes from year to year. An honest, easy-quaffing red wine at a good price. Goes well with biltong and braais.

DE WET CO-OP
PO Box 16, De Wet 6853
Tel: (0231) 92760 * Fax: (0231) 92762

You can't miss this cellar, right on the N1 highway, near to Worcester. They will rail wines to you and charge them to your credit card, which is a good, hassle-free way to keep up your stocks of everyday wines.

Sauvignon Blanc ♉♉
A well-made wine with lots of flavour at a very reasonable price.

Fernoa Pires ♉♉♉
This is a delightful and unusual off-dry wine, very spicy, with a hint of muscat honey. Good value.

Blanc de Noir ♉♉♉
A very pretty, peachy-pink wine with a lively, soft, floral fragrance and soft, fruity flavours. Understated and rather elegant. Definitely good value.

Dry Red ♉♉
If you've read this far, you'll know I like any wine with an honest name like 'Dry Red'. This one has even had a touch of wood maturation, making it quite a superior plonk. It's good to have on hand for casual guests or for any time the thirst strikes. A friendly, relaxed wine.

DIE KRANS ESTATE
PO Box 28, Calitzdorp 6660
Tel: (04437) 33314 * Fax: (04437) 33562

What a pity that Calitzdorp is so far off the beaten track for most of us plonk hunters. If you can make it, it's worth a visit. They make lovely port and other sweet wines there, and the people are friendly and welcoming. There's a Calitzdorp Port Festival at the end of each winter. Very merry and Die Krans is in the heart of the town.

Blanc de Noir ♉♉♉
This wine has a lovely salmon pink colour and sweet scent. It is made off-dry and slips down very easily. Actually, it's probably an insult to call it a plonk. Still, it's a fun wine.

DRIE BERGE PLAASKELDER
PO Box 37, Montagu 6720
Tel: (0234) 41305

This little winery seldom appears in wine guides. It's really more of a farm bottle store, but you can also buy locally made wines among the other liquors. In the informal tasting room they simply turn you loose with all the booze you can consume – wine, brandy, gin, you name it – unsupervised! On Saturday mornings a queue of farm labourers lines up to have their plastic bottles filled.

Colombard ♟♟
Rather pleasant, with some of the typical Colombard guava character, but in a subdued form.

Droë Rooi ♟♟
Definitely for early drinking. After a couple of years it loses its charm. Oh well, who needs to lay down plonk, anyway?

Grand Crû ♟
Dry and characterless, but OK in an emergency.

Late Harvest ♟♟
Quite pleasantly undemanding semi-sweet stuff. Good for an afternoon of mindless slurping while watching rugby on television.

Stein ♟
Semi-sweet and just a little sticky.

DOMEIN DOORNKRAAL
PO Box 14, De Rust 6650
Tel: (04439) 6715 * Fax: (04439) 2548

This Little Karoo farm produces ostriches and wine, and is becoming known for its rich, sweet dessert wines. It's probably a bit far for most Cape plonk drinkers to visit regularly, but it's worth getting in touch and asking for price lists. One of the fun aspects of this cellar is the names of the wines, all of which seem to have been given military rank. They're available in all sorts of sizes, from 500 ml. plastic dumpies to 10-litre drums.

Kaptein ♟♟
A blended sweet red wine, with some Chenin Blanc added to tone down the stickiness of the Red Muscadel.

Kwaaiman ♟♟
Hey, this is fun! It's a sort of medium-sweet sherry sold in a two-litre plastic container. We're moving into the *real* plonk world here.

Luitenant ♟♟♟
Rich, raisiny character with plenty of warming sweetness, but enough bite to prevent it being too jammy. Really good stuff! This will keep out the chill – even in Sutherland!

Rooikat ♟♟
A simple, semi-sweet plonk that's available in plastic bottles ranging in size from 500 ml to 10 litres! Not great, but drinkable and if you go for the giant economy pack you end up paying only R3 a litre! Beat that!

DOUGLAS CO-OP
PO Box 47, Douglas 8730
Tel: (053) 2981910 * Fax: (053) 2982445

Up there on the banks of the Orange River, this co-op makes very modestly priced wines, and is gaining a good reputation for sweet wines – understandable in all that heat.

Dry Red ♟♟
A ruby red wine with some nice fresh fruitiness. An everyday red plonk.

Fernao Pires ♟♟
This is a spicy, semi-sweet white wine that's just a little different.

Blanc de Noir ♟
A cheerful off-dry pink wine. It's not great, but it's quite drinkable.

Red Muscadel ♟♟♟
Seriously good *soetes!* And this is what you can expect from a warm region like this. The flavour is packed with gentle raisins and honey sweetness. Warming, but not too sticky. A winner!

Rosé ♟♟
A pretty, bright-pink wine with some nice strawberry scents and lots of fresh fruitiness.

Ruby Cabernet ♟♟♟
Unusually good for a plonk at this price. Quite full-bodied with lots of juicy flavour. Out of the ordinary.

Saint Anna ♟♟
A Semi-sweet, very fruity white wine.

DROSTDY-HOF WINES

Available from many bottle stores at a wide range of prices. Shop around for the best price.

Light ♟♟
A low-alcohol dry white wine. At only 9% it's probably a safe bet for a business lunch. On the other hand, you could drink grape juice and stay completely sober.

Claret Select ♟♟
A light, easy-drinking red plonk. Fruity and fresh, and even a touch of wood.

Late Harvest ♟♟
A semi-sweet white wine. Bland, but pleasant.

Stein Select ♟♟
A pleasant, but unspectacular semi-sweet white wine for casual drinking or cooking. Good over crushed ice as a summer drink.

DU TOITSKLOOF CO-OP
PO Box 55, Rawsonville 6845
Tel: (0231) 91601 * Fax: (0231) 91581

It's such a pity they moved the N1! It used to go right past this winery. Now you have to do a little detour, which is certainly worth the effort. They are happy to rail wines to you and charge it to your credit card account. Phone for their price list and order form.

Riesling ♟♟
A delicate and fruity dry white wine.

Sauvignon Blanc ♟♟♟
Very dry, but full of clean, fresh flavour and an attractive grassy nose.

Weisser Riesling 🍷🍷
Made off-dry, this wine has a nice spicy nose.

Bukkettraube 🍷🍷
A semi-sweet white wine with the fragrance of rose petals and blossoms. Very pleasant with Thai food or babotie.

Red Jeripigo 🍷🍷🍷
If you're going canoeing on the Berg River, don't set off without a bottle of this delicious distilled sunshine. It will warm the chilliest of paddlers.

Shiraz 🍷🍷
A warming red wine, full of spice and old-leather fragrance. The sort of wine that goes well with a crackling fire and a good book, or a friend and a game of chess.

Vino Uno wines 🍷🍷
Packed in 500 ml screw-cap dumpy bottles, these are fun wines for everyday braaiing and picnicking. Very good value. There's a Dry Red (light and easy), a Semi-sweet White (pleasant, flowery bouquet) and a Dry White (light and crisp).

ECLIPSE WINES
The Wine Warehouse, Ravenscraig Road, Woodstock 7925
Tel: (021) 4482371

Wine merchant Oscar Foulkes has impressed wine-lovers everywhere with his range of personally selected designer wines at very modest prices. They are available from the Shoprite/Checkers group of supermarkets, as well as from Macro and his own Wine Warehouse in Woodstock.

Dry Red 🍷🍷🍷
This superb blend of Shiraz and Cabernet is smooth and easy-to-drink and has plenty of complex character. Stunning value!

Eclipse Sauvignon Blanc 🍷🍷
A clean, fresh dry white wine to accompany a meal of grilled fish.

Eclipse Stein ♟♟♟
An easy-drinking, relaxed style semi-sweet wine for casual enjoyment. Not your usual bland 'stein' sold in boxes. This one's special.

Eclipse Minuet ♟♟
A charming off-dry wine for year-round drinking pleasure. Undemanding and friendly.

Mystery Vivaldi ♟♟♟
This stunning red wine has loads of ripe berry flavours and complex, spicy aromas. Incredible value for money.

Mystery Dry White ♟♟
This changes from time to time, according to what Oscar finds in his exploration of the Cape's cellars. Always good value.

Oscar's Reserve ♟♟♟
Another winner from this selection and much more than just a plonk. This is an elegant wine blended from Shiraz and Cabernet, with a touch of subtle wood.

EERSTERIVIER KELDER
PO Box 2, Vlottenburg 7604
Tel: (021) 8813870 * Fax: (021) 8813102

Dedicated plonk drinkers have come to rely on this cellar, quite close to Stellenbosch, for their everyday, reliable quaffing wines. The Le Foyer range of braai wines is sold only at the co-op and represents excellent value for money. Eersterivier produces some very acceptable and elegant wines.

Hanseret Claret ♟♟
A nice, light, earthy dry red wine with an honest flavour to it. It's even been given some oak maturation.

Le Foyer Dry Red ♟♟
This wine is gently fruity, light-bodied and slips down very well. The winemaker calls it the 'sportsman's companion'.

Le Foyer Dry White ♟♟
An undemanding but reliable everyday wine.

Le Foyer Late Vintage ♟♟
Sweetish and a little sticky for my palate. I'm told it's popular at student braais.

Pinotage ♟♟♟
A deliciously clean dry red wine without the added complication of wood. Easy drinking and excellent value.

Muscat d'Alexandrie ♟♟
A very unusual semi-sweet white wine that's immensely popular with up-country visitors. Lots of honey fragrance, but not too sticky sweet.

EIKENDAL VINEYARDS
PO Box 2261, Dennesig 7601
Tel: (024) 551422 * Fax: (024) 551027

This is a very attractive modern cellar, not far from Somerset West on the Stellenbosch road, produces some really great wines which are often overlooked by wine lovers. They serve fine Swiss country lunches in summer and fondues in winter. Most of the wines are far too elegant and refined to be classed as plonks, but try this one.

Rouge ♟♟♟
A good honest red wine blended from several cultivars. Nice and fruity and light enough to drink all day.

GOLDEN ALABAMA ♟

This popular wine comes in several sizes and is a really big seller in some areas. Up-market liquor stores don't display it very prominently. Don't look among the vintage Cabernets. You'll probably find it tucked away on the bottom shelf. No problem. Regular customers will know exactly where to find it. Made for the mass market, Golden Alabama has been given a brownish, amber colour, which leads one to expect a sweetish wine, but it's actually quite dry. It's a thinnish wine with not much character, but a good price! Ice would help, but is not traditionally used by Golden Alabama drinkers.

FAIRVIEW ESTATE
PO Box 583, Suider Paarl 7625
Tel: (02211) 632450 * Fax: (02211) 632591

Summer tourists stop here to admire the goats, but wine lovers know there are always bargains to be found. There are also always new and unusual wines from Charles Back's innovative cellar. Several fall into our plonk price category, although none of them could be described as cheap and nasty. Great wines!

Gamay Noir ♀♀♀
One of the best of the Nouveau-style young wines. Drier than most, but deliciously fruity and quite soft on the palate. Good summer enjoyment.

Zinfandel-Cinsaut Blend ♀♀♀
A really exciting new blend. You won't find one like it anywhere else. A deliciously complex red wine, but be careful of the alcohol. At 14,5% it could kick like Joel Stransky.

Dry Rosé ♀♀
Rosé wines should be far more popular in our hot climate than they are. This one makes for perfect summer sipping. Fruity and clean.

Bouquet Fair ♀♀♀
A very fragrant, soft-drinking off-dry wine with spice and fruit on the palate. Delicious.

Sauvignon Blanc-Chenin Blanc ♀♀♀
A dry white wine with loads of crisp fruit. Big, juicy and mouth-filling. Great stuff!

Chenin Blanc ♀♀
his wine has a gentle, fruit salad and blossoms nose, very juicy on the tongue. Excellent with food.

FRANSCHHOEK VINEYARDS CO-OP
PO Box 52, Franschhoek 7690
Tel: (02212) 2086 * Fax: (02212) 3440

This fast-growing co-op has been in existence for 50 years and makes La Cotte wines. They also produce wines under private labels for individual members. Several of their wines are sold in handy 500 ml bottles – always a plus for plonk lovers. And if you're feeling rich, buy a bottle of their delicious La Cotte Port. It's one of the best.

Blanc de Blanc ♗♗
A very pleasant, light dry white wine with clean, citrus character. Perfect for summer. It's also available in 500 ml bottles.

Sémillon ♗♗
It's good to see a co-op marketing Sémillon. This wine will become increasingly popular, mark my words! This one is dry and fresh, crisply fruity.

Grand Rouge ♗♗♗
A cheerful, well-balanced dry red wine made mostly from Cinsaut. Easy-drinking, excellent value.

Claret ♗♗
Sold in 500ml dumpie bottles, this is a very pleasant little wine to have in your rucksack or on a boat. Great little price, too!

Sémillon Semi-sweet ♗♗
Available in normal sized bottles or 500 ml ones, this unusual wine is made off-dry and has some lovely fruit salad flavours and a nice tropical fruit scent. Good value.

Hanepoot ♗♗
Good to find a fortified, sweet wine at a sensible price. Sweet and grapey, with nice muscat scents and honey flavours.

GOUDINI CO-OP
PO Box 132, Rawsonville 6845
Tel: (0231) 91090 * Fax: (0231) 91095

They make some very pleasant wines at this co-op and sell them at remarkably reasonable prices. They also produce wines in five-litre boxes. Great value plonks. And they're geared up to rail wines anywhere.

Steen Late Harvest ♗♗♗
A gentle, peach flavoured wine, easy-drinking, semi-sweet and with quite a low alcohol content.

Steen ♗♗
A good old South African name for Chenin Blanc. Dry, but with some fruit salad fragrance. It's reliable and inexpensive.

Clairette Blanche ♟♟
An everyday, easy-sipping dry white wine with quite a lot of character.

Ruby Cabernet ♟♟
A pretty ruby colour with some nice juicy fruitiness. Very smooth.

GROOT EILAND CO-OP
PO Box 93, Rawsonville 6845
Tel: (0231) 91140 * Fax: (0231) 91801

This little co-op has climbed onto the tourist bandwagon and is providing typical Breede River braais and potjiekos meals to go with the wines.

Cabernet Sauvignon ♟♟
Well, well! A Cabernet at a plonk price! Actually, it's quite an uncomplicated dry red wine. Not great, but certainly good enough for relaxed drinking.

Riesling ♟♟
Not as bland as many Cape Rieslings, this one has some nice crisp fruitiness. Easy drinking.

Laatoes ♟♟
An uncomplicated semi-sweet Chenin Blanc. Quite fruity.

HEERENHOF WINES

This range is made by Douglas Green Bellingham.

Dry Red ♟♟
Made from Cinsaut, soft and very quaffable. A rather pleasant little plonk. Lightish alcohol.

Grand Crû ♟♟
A pleasant, undemanding dry white wine. Unpretentious, but perfectly drinkable.

Late Harvest ♟♟
Semi-sweet and fruity, but not too sticky.

Honey Blossom 🍷🍷
A low-priced semi-sweet white wine that's extremely popular in some down-market areas. Made of Chenin Blanc, it's quite smooth. Not great, but very consistent quality. The customers demand it! It's usually bought in litre bottles or two-litre jugs. Regulars say 750 ml bottles are for sissies.

HUGUENOT WINES
PO Box 275, Wellington 7655
Tel: (02211) 641277 * Fax: (02211) 32075

This is a private wholesale company that blends and markets its own range of reasonably priced wines. Some are sold in 750 ml bottles and others in five-litre boxes. The cellar is not open to the public, but you could phone and find out about your nearest stockist.

Blanc de Noir 🍷🍷
A pale pink wine with a soft, fruity nose, but a surprisingly dry flavour. Pleasant and simple.

Smooth Red 🍷🍷
Light ruby colour. A blend of Cinsaut and Pinotage. Nicely fruity and dry for everyday, easy-drinking. An honest wine.

Valentine Cerise 🍷🍷
A sweetish, pink sparkling wine that looks pretty on a party table. It's okay for a special breakfast too.

Zellerhof Late Harvest 🍷🍷
A semi-sweet white wine in a five-litre box. Quite fruity but not memorable. Reasonable value.

Zellerhof Premier Grand Crû 🍷🍷
Five litres of very dry white wine. Not a great deal of character, but certainly acceptable for casual quaffing.

KAAPZICHT ESTATE
PO Box 5, Sanlamhof 7532
Tel: (021) 9033870 * Fax: (021) 9036272

This Stellenbosch estate, with its spectacular view of Table Mountain, employs casual pickers during the harvest. Many regulars come all the way from the Free State to help bring in the grapes. What a way to spend a holiday!

Dry White ♟♟
This dry, everyday plonk is sold in a five-litre bag-in-a-box. Honest, basic stuff, easy to drink and not difficult to pay for either.

Kaapblanc ♟♟
A dry white wine made mainly from Colombard. It has some nice fruit salad scents and juicy flavour.

Kaaproodt ♟♟
A plain, everyday red wine sold in a five-litre bag-in-a-box. Convenient and pleasantly fruity.

KANGO CO-OP
PO Box 46, Oudtshoorn 6620
Tel: (0443) 226065 * Fax: (0443) 291038

It is only relatively recently that parts of Oudtshoorn have switched from apple farming to grapes, which seem to thrive in the usually hot, dry area. Unusual to find vines and a winery so far from the rest of the Cape's wine world. They'll rail wine to you if you order a minimum of two cartons and will make up assorted lots too.

Chardonnay ♟♟
A light and dry Chardonnay, unwooded, with a mild lemon tang.

Sauvignon Blanc ♟♟
A crisp, grassy white wine, dry, but quite fruity. Light alcohol and clean character.

Xandre ♟♟
Light and off-dry for easy quaffing.

Herfsgoud ♟♟
Rather a pleasing semi-sweet white wine with warm honey flavours.

Blanc de Noir ♀♀♀
Light coloured, fragrant, off-dry and quite fruity. A relaxed, light-bodied wine for summer.

Claret ♀♀♀
A very light coloured red wine, almost a Rosé. It has soft summer scents and a touch of sweetness on the tongue. Unusual and pleasant. Should be served quite cool.

Red Muscadel ♀♀♀
This is more the sort of wine you'd expect from an area like this! Warming and rich, with nice raisins and honey flavours.

White Muscadel ♀♀♀
Very similar in style to the above. Sweet and comfortable.

KELLERPRINZ WINES

Available from most bottle stores, these are old favourites with plonk drinkers. Kellerprinz is the SFW's oldest budget priced range and the wines are always reliable. Quality control of these wines is very strict.

Grand Crû ♀♀
A fresh dry white wine made of a blend of Chenin Blanc and Colombard. Good value.

Late Harvest ♀♀
A semi-sweet white wine. Always reliable, easy to drink and packed with ripe fruity sweetness.

Rosanne ♀♀
A pretty semi-sweet Rosé wine with a mouth-filling, fruity flavour and a nice balance. Cheerful drinking for a party.

Selected Stein ♀♀
A semi-sweet, plain and unpretentious white wine.

KLAWER CO-OP
PO Box 8, Klawer 8145
Tel: (02724) 61530 * Fax: (02724) 61561

This co-op seems to do very well at regional and national wine shows and has produced some very pleasant wines.

Blanc de Blanc ♟♟
Made just off-dry, this white wine has a gentle fruitiness in the background.

Blanc de Noir ♟♟♟
An excellent everyday semi-sweet pink wine.

Late Vintage ♟♟
A blended, low-alcohol semi-sweet white wine made from Colombard and Chenin Blanc – a hint of guava on the nose and a touch of clean acidity.

Michelle Vin Doux ♟
Unusual. A light pink bubbly, sweet and jolly. Fine for parties, but rather sticky.

Premier Grand Crû ♟♟
A very dry white wine, light-bodied and smooth. Undemanding for everyday drinking.

Red Muscadel ♟♟♟
A lovely wine with honey and raisins on the nose and lots of rich, sweet fruitiness as it slips down. Leave this for a year and it will be stunning!

Cape Riesling ♟♟
An unspectacular, clean, refreshing dry white wine.

Vin Rouge ♟♟
An easy-drinking, honest dry red wine with a touch of subtle wood and some fruitiness. Good value.

KOELENHOF CO-OP
PO Box 1, Koelenhof 7605
Tel: (021) 8822020 * Fax: (021) 8822796

While most of the wine from this co-op goes to the big wholesalers, they do keep some for sale to visitors and will rail wines to customers.

Koelenberg ♟♟
A soft, easy-drinking, blended dry red wine that is very user-friendly and versatile.

Pinotage Rosé ΨΨΨ
A very attractive pink wine with wafts of fresh strawberry scents on the nose and lots of lively, freshly-picked fruit flavour. A delicious drink with cold ham and salads.

Koelenhoffer ΨΨ
A clean, dry white wine blended from Sauvignon Blanc and Chenin Blanc. Uncomplicated.

Special Late Harvest ΨΨ
Nice rose scented wine made of Gewurztraminer. Semi-sweet and very nicely balanced.

Koelenheimer ΨΨ
This juicy semi-sweet white wine benefits from a touch of Hanepoot (don't we all?).

Sweet Hanepoot ΨΨ
Now this is the real *soetes*. Honey flavoured and mouthfilling. Good warming stuff!

Steen Jerepigo ΨΨΨ
Wonderful summer fruits on the nose and big, rich honey and fruit flavours nicely balanced by a touch of fresh acid. An orgasmic experience for a sweet wine devotee.

LADISMITH CO-OP
PO Box 56, Ladismith 6885
Tel: (028) 5511042 * Fax: (028) 5511930

At this Little Karoo co-op they distil brandy, so it is only when the grapes are exceptional that they save them for making wine. They must have been quite exceptional recently, because they've exported some to Switzerland. The list of wines changes considerably from year to year.

Aristaat ΨΨ
A pleasant dry white, blended wine.

Chenin Blanc ΨΨ
A dry white wine with no fancy pretentions. Some fruitiness.

Stein ΨΨ
An honest, straight-forward semi-sweet white wine for casual drinking.

Soet Hanepoot ♟♟♟
Available in two-litre and five-litre returnable containers. And you get your money back for the can when you come for a refill. This sunny sweet wine is a plonk drinker's dream. Just right as a last glass before bed.

LANDSKROON ESTATE
PO Box 519, Suider Paarl 7624
Tel: (02211) 631039 * Fax: (02211) 632810

This Paarl estate, more than 300 years old, is famous for its good red wines of elegance. It's nice to know that some of their wines are available at plonk prices.

Blanc de Noir ♟♟
A pale, orange-pink wine with a softly floral nose and a very smooth, gentle character. Off-dry and easy. Well worth trying.

Landskroon Dry Red ♟♟
Very reasonably priced for a wood-matured red blend. Smooth and fruity. Grab some when you're in the area.

Chenin Blanc ♟♟
They make this in a semi-sweet and a dry version. Try them both, they're easy to drink.

LANDZICHT CO-OP
PO Box 94, Jacobsdal 8710
Tel: (053212) 132 * Fax: (053212) 113

Well, a winery up in the Free State! Whatever next! It's unusual to have wine grapes in a summer rainfall area, but these seem to have a loyal following.

Rose ♟♟
A blend of Pinotage with white wine grapes, Colombard and Hanepoot. Sweetish, but with quite a clean finish.

Rein Blum ♟♟
A blend of several varieties of white grape, made off-dry and slightly spicy. Quite fresh and user-friendly.

Nagmaalwyn 🍷🍷
You don't have to be religious to enjoy this raisin-sweet red muscadel. A warming drink for a chilly Free State night.

Rouge du Bois 🍷🍷
A well-priced, wood-matured dry red wine for easy quaffing.

Late Harvest 🍷🍷
A pleasantly semi-sweet white wine with some fresh, grassy aromas and a touch of honey achieved by adding Hanepoot.

Stein 🍷🍷
A soft, understated semi-sweet white wine.

LANGVERWACHT CO-OP
PO Box 87, Bonnievale 6730
Tel: (02346) 2815 * Fax: (02346) 3059

They make very small quantities of wine for sale from the cellar and these are mostly sold by mail order, so send for a price list.

Blanc de Blanc 🍷🍷
A dry white wine, blended from Colombar and Chenin Blanc, and a very popular seller. Light in body, with fresh clean acidity. Very good value.

Colombard 🍷🍷
Always a good bet in this area. This one is made dry, but has a nice guava and herb fragrance and fruity character.

Hanepoot Jerepigo 🍷🍷🍷
A good, sweet fortified wine, packed with the flavour of very ripe grapes. Very complex. Excellent for winter.

Late Harvest 🍷🍷
A rather light, perfumed wine made from Chenin Blanc. Quite pretty and easy-drinking. Semi-sweet.

Sauvignon Blanc 🍷🍷
A fresh grassy nose and some nice herbal flavours make this a good value for money wine. Clean and refreshing.

LANZERAC (Made by SFW)

The Lanzerac range of wines is gaining popularity again, but those tear-drop shaped bottles are a bit difficult to store in your wine shelves. Most of them have moved out of the plonk category.

Rosé ♟♟
One of the few local rosé wines made by blending red and white wine. A semi-sweet pink wine with a fresh, dry finish. Goes well with spare ribs.

LATEGANSKOP CO-OP
PO Box 44, Breërivier 6858
Tel and Fax: (02324) 719

This new co-op, about a kilometre from Bergsig Estate, has just three wines on the wine list, but they're worth tasting and not expensive.

Merlot ♟♟
An unwooded dry red wine made in 1993 in a light, easy-drinking style. You could lay this one down for a few years and it might become quite spectacular.

Pinotage ♟♟
A very drinkable fruity dry red wine at about R7 a bottle. Excellent to keep on hand as a house plonk.

Port ♟♟
A pleasant, juicy port. Good to have a port at a plonk price.

LIEBERSTEIN ♟♟
This is the wine that launched plonk drinking in South Africa. Before Lieberstein came on the scene, wine drinkers were either rich and pretentious or poor and scruffy. Lieberstein bounced in as the 'anywhere, any time' wine to be enjoyed by ordinary people. It is an unpretentious semi-sweet white wine that's very easy to drink. Serve chilled in a decanter and you'll impress even your most pretentious sipper friends.

LIEVLAND ESTATE
PO Box 66, Klapmuts 7625
Tel: (02211) 5226 * Fax: (02211) 5213

This remarkable estate has achieved amazing results with red wines. Every red wine produced by cellar master Abe Beukes has won an award!

Cheandrie ♟♟
An off-dry, blended white wine that needs no explanation. Just open it and drink it on the stoep on a sunny day. Fruity and well balanced.

Lievlander ♟♟♟
A good value blended red wine that has been selected by wine clubs in blind tastings, competing against wines at far higher prices. Smooth and fruity. A winner.

LOUWSHOEK-VOORSORG CO-OP
PO Box 174, Rawsonville 6845
Tel and Fax: (0231) 91110

This enterprising little co-op sells most of its wines to big merchants, but they make some very interesting wines for local sale too. Slightly beyond the plonk range is their Nectar de Provision, a sweet fortified red wine, well worth trying. They are happy to rail wines to customers.

Premier Grand Cru ♟♟
A light, crisp dry white wine to enjoy with grilled fish on a hot day.

Chardonnay ♟♟♟
A relative newcomer to this cellar, with fresh citrus flavours, tangy and tasty. Very good value.

Riesling ♟♟
An earthy, slightly acid dry white wine. Good with slightly oily food.

Chenin Blanc ♟♟♟
A nicely balanced semi-sweet white wine with scents of summer fruit salad for everyday enjoyment.

Dry Red ♟♟
A hearty, fruity red wine for easy quaffing any old time.

LUTZVILLE CO-OP
PO Box 50, Lutzville 8165
Tel: (02725) 71516 * Fax: (02725) 71435

This winery, on the outskirts of Lutzville in the lower regions of the Olifants River, uses most of its grapes to make grape juice concentrate. Some however, is made into good wines, most of which are sold under the Fleermuisklip (Bat Rock) label. They are happy to rail wines anywhere and will even send off mixed cases.

Fleermuisklip Grand Crû ♟♟
A dry, full-bodied white wine with a touch of acidity. Reliable and unpretentious.

Fleermuisklip Sauvignon Blanc ♟♟
A crisp white wine. Not much of the typical Sauvignon character, but undemanding.

Fleermuisklip Bukettraube ♟♟
An off-dry white without much character.

Fleermuisklip Late Harvest ♟♟
Sweet and juicy, this should go quite well with bobotie or a mild curry. Along the west coast, they probably enjoy it with their kreef.

Fleermuisklip Robyn ♟♟
Quite a pleasant dry red table wine, without much pretension. Full of flavour and good for drinking at any time.

Lutzville Wingerde Soet Hanepoot ♟♟
A quite delicate, sweet fortified wine, with the honey muscat character kept very subtle.

MAMREWEG CO-OP
PO Box 114, Darling 7345
Tel: (02241) 2276 * Fax: (02241) 2647

Mamreweg wines are becoming freely available as more and more liquor stores discover their value. They're modestly priced and drinkable.

Blanc de Blanc ♟♟♟
A fresh, crisp dry white wine with mouth-filling character and a nice touch of fruitiness to add interest. Very good value. This is a wine that could impress your up-market friends if you serve it from a smart decanter.

Blanc de Noir ♟♟
A pretty peachy-pink colour and quite a nice touch of fruitiness here. Just right for a casual party.

Chenin Blanc ♟♟♟
A soft, easy-drinking off-dry white wine with an attractive flower-petal nose. Really good value.

Cinsaut ♟♟♟
A very honest, slightly earthy wine for everyday quaffing. Lots of sweet fruit and amazingly good value. An old favourite of mine.

Claret ♟♟
A remarkably good red wine made from Tinta Barocca and Pinotage. Light-bodied, fruity and cheerful. Perfect with mutton chops.

Colombard ♟♟
A lively, full-bodied off-dry wine with a nice balance between sweetness and acidity.

Dry Steen ♟♟
A dry white wine with hints of guava on the nose. It could go well with a fish braai.

Late Harvest ♟♟
Quite a sweet white wine made from Chenin Blanc. Fruity and pleasant. Serve chilled or even over crushed ice.

Pinotage ♟♟♟
A very pleasant red wine, medium-bodied and fruity, with some typical Pinotage character. Certainly much improved since I last tasted it.

Riesling ♟♟
A very clean, crisp dry white wine with a flowery nose. It should appeal to quite sophisticated palates. Wonderful with chicken dishes.

Special Late Harvest ♟♟
Some pleasant summer fruit scents in this wine, followed by fruit salad sweetness and lots of juicy succulence. A nice clean ending.

Stein ♟♟
A very easy-drinking semi-sweet Chenin Blanc with some pawpaw scents and good fruity flavours. A nice crisp finish.

Tinta Barocca ♟♟♟
Fruity and light, but you can taste why this is a favourite port wine grape. Made for early drinking, this is a good casual drink, like most of the Mamreweg wines.

McGREGOR CO-OP
Private Bag X619, Robertson 6705
Tel: (02353) 741 * Fax: (02353) 829

McGregor is one of those trendy little towns that attracts Cape Town pensioners and those who can afford weekend retreats. The wines from the co-op are very modestly priced and nicely labelled as souvenirs, with village scenes and tartan tops. McGregor folk regard their local co-op with loyal affection, and no wonder.

Cabernet Sauvignon ♟♟
Made in a roughish style, this is a casual Cabernet with no aspirations to greatness. It could mellow with time. Good accompaniment to rich stews or ox-tail casserole.

Late Vintage Steen ♟♟
A semi-sweet white wine with an old-fashioned name. Juicy and fruity, good value.

Colombard ♟♟♟
As one would expect of a Colombard from this area, this is excellent. Made just off-dry, but very clean and refreshing. The ideal wine for summer.

Late Vintage ♟♟
A blossom and honey bouquet, sweet fruitiness and some acidity to balance it all. A very pleasant wine indeed.

Red Muscadel ♟♟
A lovely rich red-amber wine with raisin sweetness. Splendid at the end of a good meal.

Port ♟♟
An unusually dry port made from Cabernet. Should be great in a few years' time, but not really together yet. At this price, lay some down.

MERWESPONT CO-OP
PO Box 68, Bonnievale 6730
Tel: (02346) 2800 * Fax: (02346) 2734

This is a small, quite informal co-op, but they produce some friendly wines at equally friendly prices. Not a vast range.

Cabernet Sauvignon ♅♅
A recent addition to the range. Quite a simple, straight-forward, unwooded dry red wine. Pleasant for everyday drinking and very modestly priced.

Blanc de Blanc ♅♅
A light-bodied dry white wine with a shy hint of guavas on the nose. Subtle and gentle.

Late Vintage ♅♅
Very subtle nose and some rather nice ripe fruitiness make this semi-sweet wine a good, smooth drink.

Vin Rosé ♅♅
A rather pleasant little semi-sweet pink wine, with a tingle of very small bubbles. Fresh and juicy – actually very refreshing if served chilled.

MERWIDA CO-OP
PO Box 4, Rawsonville 6845
Tel: (0231) 91144 * Fax: (0231) 91953

This little co-op near Rawsonville is owned by two Van der Merwe families who are fifth-generation wine farmers. It produces about six thousand cases of wine a year. Inexpensive and reasonable quality. They'll rail wine to you.

Ruby Cabernet ♅♅
A nice, medium-bodied, unwooded red wine with some pleasant fruitiness and a lingering finish. Quite a serious wine.

Chenin Blanc ♅♅
A sound, no frills semi-sweet white wine for every day enjoyment.

Colombard ♅♅
Made just off-dry, this is an easy quaffing wine to enjoy alfresco.

Chardonnay ⚏
It's good to discover a Chardonnay at a plonk price! This one is light and lemony and has none of the buttery vanilla flavour you get from wood maturation.

Sauvignon Blanc ⚏
A very reasonably priced dry white wine, with some pleasant summer fruit flavours and a clean finish. Great with calamari.

MONS RUBER ESTATE
Private Bag X629, Oudtshoorn 6620
Tel and Fax: (04439) 6550

The Little Karoo is fast establishing a name for itself as a serious wine producing area, especially in the field of good Port. This is likely to become the 'Duoro Valley' of South Africa. They make several good table wines too.

Conari ⚏⚏⚏
A very pleasant Cabernet Sauvignon without any wood maturation, but plenty of rich berry flavours and a nice spicy nose. A serious wine at a reasonable price.

Elegantia ⚏
A fruity sweet Muscadel Jerepigo with lots of honey and raisins in the flavour.

Vino ⚏
A simple name for an unusual wine. Probably the only dry wine made from Muscadel grapes! Made to be drunk early. Full of honey scents.

MONTAGU CO-OP
PO Box 29, Montagu 6720
Tel: (0234) 41125 * Fax: (0234) 41793

Although most of their wine is sold to the big wholesale merchants, some good honest wines can be found at this co-op, and it's well worth a visit if you're in the area. It's a good source of soetes, but there's much more than that to discover. They'll happily rail wine to you.

Chenin Blanc ⚏
A regular dry white table wine for easy quaffing. Well balanced.

Colombar ♟♟
Off-dry in a popular soft style for relaxed drinking.

Mont Blanc ♟♟♟
An off-dry white wine made from Muscadel grapes, picked very young. This gives it an unexpected crispness, alongside the honey sweetness.

Late Vintage ♟♟
A pleasant semi-sweet wine with the fragrance of blossoms and lots of juicy fruitiness. Some acidity gives it a clean, refreshing finish.

MONTEREY WINES

Boxed wines from Western Province Cellars.

Late Harvest ♟♟
A semi-sweet white wine with flowery nose and lots of fruit and honey sweetness. Slightly cloying, but fine for the first glass or two.

Premier Grand Crû ♟♟
A clean, fruity, soft dry white wine with not too much acid.

Rouge ♟♟
A smooth dry red with some ripe-fig flavours and pleasant nose. Fruity and mouth-filling.

Stein ♟♟
Fruit salad sweetness on the nose and some fresh fruit on the palate.

MOOIUITSIG WYNKELDERS
PO Box 15, Bonnievale 6730
Tel: (02346) 2143 * Fax: (02346) 2675

This is actually a large liquor wholesaler, probably the largest privately owned one in the country. They produce several wines under the Ouderust, Slabbers and Mooiuitsig labels.

Ouderust Colombard ♟♟
An off-dry white wine with soft, fruit salad flavours and a sweetish finish.

Rusthof Dry Red ♟♟
A fruity red wine that has an almost sweet flavour, but a clean dry finish. Pleasant and good value.

Slabbers Old Brown Sherry ♟♟
Very reasonably priced. Dark and sweet – ideal for winter warmth, or to take on a fishing trip.

Slabbers Golden Hanepoot ♟♟♟
A *soetes* for the connoisseur, with big, honey flavours and some spicy undertones. Sweet and warming.

Mooiuitsig Old Brown Sherry ♟♟
Standard fare for certain rock fishermen. A bottle is an essential part of the tackle. Keeps any angler warm.

Mooiuitsig Invalid Port ♟♟
You don't even have to be an invalid to enjoy this warming wine. A comfortable finish to a good meal.

NORDALE CO-OP
PO Box 105, Bonnievale 6730
Tel: (02346) 2050 * Fax: (02346) 2192

As with many co-ops, most of this cellar's production goes to large merchant wholesalers, but some are available under their own label.

Colombar ♟♟
A very gentle, soft white wine for easy quaffing. Rather more subtle than most Colombars. It's dry, but there's just a hint of sweetness in the background.

Dry Red ♟♟♟
An interesting, soft and smooth dry red. Very flavourful for a red plonk. Light enough to sip well chilled in summer.

Red Muscadel Jerepigo ♟♟♟
Very juicy, smooth sweet wine, full of summer fragrance and honey-and-raisin richness. This wine is a real winner.

NUY WYNKELDER
PO Box 5225, Worcester 6851
Tel: (0231) 70272 * Fax: (0231) 74994

This award-winning co-op has produced some of the Cape's top Muscadels and is winning prizes all the way. No wonder the winemaker, Wilhelm Linder, was twice selected as Winemaker of the Year.

Rouge de Nuy ♀♀♀
An easy-drinking red with a spicy, smokey nose and lots of juicy sweetness on the palate, followed by a clean, lingering finish. Definitely a super-plonk.

Riesling ♀♀
A clean, fruity dry white wine for any old time.

Colombard ♀♀♀
An unusually dry Colombard, clean and fruity. One of the country's nicest Colombards. (Nuy also makes a semi-sweet Colombard – pleasant, but not as spectacular as the dry one.)

Chant de Nuit ♀♀
This is something very different. The addition of a small quantity of the table grape, Ferdinant de Lesseps, gives it a distinctive pineapple aroma. This is a delicious wine.

Fernao Pirez ♀♀
A very light, off-dry white wine with teasingly spicy flavours.

Bukettraube ♀♀
An elegant, off-dry white wine with subtle rose-petal scents and honey muscat flavours.

Steen ♀♀
A sunny, semi-sweet wine with plenty of summer fruit in the flavour.

OOM TAS ♀♀
This amber coloured semi-sweet wine has a loyal following and claims to be one of the biggest sellers in South Africa. The colouring is added to a Blanc de Noir wine and if you taste it without seeing the amber colour, you'll probably be very impressed. Still, the colour is important to Oom Tas drinkers, so it's there to stay.

ORANJERIVIER WYNKELDERS
PO Box 544, Upington 8800
Tel: (054) 25651 * Fax: (054) 25408

A bit out of the way for your ordinary wine route fan, but this is the largest co-op in South Africa.

Ruby Cabernet ♟♟
A very soft, smooth plonk for everyday quaffing.

Bonne Souvenir ♟♟
A slightly heavier red, also mainly Ruby Cabernet. Good with steak.

Blanc de Noir ♟♟
Ruby Cabernet again – they must have plenty up there! This time a pale, peachy colour and some dried-fruit sweetness.

Chenin Blanc ♟♟
A fresh, fruity white wine for everyday dopping.

Colombard ♟♟
A nicely balanced, fruity wine with a sweet character and good acid balance.

Dry Red ♟♟
Plain and quite drinkable, a red plonk made from Pinotage and – you guessed – Ruby Cabernet.

Grand Crû ♟
A very dry white wine, suitable for cooking.

Jerepigo ♟♟
Good, warming stuff! Brownish colour and sweet sultana scents and flavours. Just the thing to keep out the winter chills.

Late Harvest ♟♟
This fruity and semi-sweet wine is a pleasant accompaniment to dried fruit grown in this hot area. Serve well chilled.

Red Muscadel ♟♟♟
The warmth of the Orange River area makes it ideal for the production of full-sweet wines like this. Raisiny and rich. Good stuff!

Rosé ♟♟
A pretty pink wine, delicate and semi-sweet. Quite pleasantly fruity. Definitely a party wine. Serve well chilled.

OVERHEX CO-OP
PO Box 139, Worcester 6849
Tel and Fax: (0231) 71057

This cellar has been modernized and given a new look. It's worth a visit if you're up that way. They produce handy three-bottle gift packs and will rail wines to you.

Clairette Blanche
A dry white wine with plenty of mouth-filling flavour and body. Quite a serious wine at a frivolous price.

Colombar
A semi-sweet white wine with some nice fruit salad aroma and a low alcohol content.

Riesling
Scents of straw and not much fruit on this dry white wine. Not a bad accompaniment to a mussel stew.

OVERMEER WINES

This range of boxed wines is produced by SFW, who say it's the best selling boxed wine in the country. The Late Harvest is the most popular wine in the range. They're very reasonably priced. At 11 percent alcohol, most of them are excellent for daytime quaffing.

Grand Crû
A dry wine, with a touch of fruit in the background. Makes a nice spritzer.

Red
A dry red, soft and quite smooth, for easy, uncomplicated drinking. Good accompaniment to mindless TV watching on a wet day.

Late Harvest
A semi-sweet white wine with plenty of juicy fruit flavours. Great for washing down samoosas.

Stein
An off-dry white wine with a nice sugar-acid balance. Try this with spare ribs.

PAARL PERLÉ 🍷🍷
A legendary wine, semi-sweet and with a slight prickle of bubbles. A hint of Hanepoot gives it a nice honey flavour. Its fans love it, while its detractors declare that there's a headache in every bottle. Actually, it's a harmless enough wine and not bad value. For some strange reason it's not available in the Western Cape. Oh well, I suppose the Gautengis have to have SOME wines of their own.

PERDEBERG CO-OP
PO Box 214, Paarl 7620
Tel: (02211) 638112 * Fax: (02211) 638245

Wine prices at this co-op are extremely reasonable. A plonk-lover's dream! And the wines are not at all bad, either. It's worth getting to know them better.

Cinsaut 🍷🍷
Cinsaut makes light fruity wines for easy and early drinking, and this one's no exception. It's easy on the pocket too. A pizza wine.

Pinotage 🍷🍷🍷
A very juicy, everyday red wine with not too much tannin or acid. Easy-drinking and friendly.

Chenin Blanc 🍷🍷
They make two versions of this versatile wine here at Perdeberg; one is dry and the other semi-sweet. Take your pick. They're both lekker.

Colombar 🍷🍷
A quite fruity dry white wine with some fruit salad and guava scents. Excellent value.

Late Vintage 🍷🍷
Made from Chenin Blanc, this wine has a nice, fruit salad character, for those who like their wine a little sweeter. It goes well with curries or on its own. Good value.

PICARDI NAKED TRUTH WINES ♀♀♀
Available at Picardi Liquor Stores. These very plain bottles don't have any brand names on them. All you see is a little sticker saying 'Dry Red' or 'Dry White'. Try them, they're really good. Great value.

PICK 'N PAY WINES–Ravenswood.

House brands can be excellent value, but they can also vary in quality from batch to batch. The five-litre Ravenswood wines we tasted were not great. The smaller 500 ml tetrapaks were far better. Maybe ours was just a bad batch.

Ravenswood Dry Red ♀
A roughish red wine, rather tart and lacking fruit.

Ravenswood Late Harvest ♀♀
An unspectacular semi-sweet white wine with fruit salad flavours.

Ravenswood Premier Grand Crû ♀♀
A very dry white wine with some fruity aromas.

Ravenswood Selected Stein ♀♀
A very straight forward semi-sweet white wine with a hint of honey in the flavour. This might go well with curry and rice.

PORTERVILLE CO-OP
PO Box 52, Porterville 6810
Tel: (02623) 2170 * Fax: (02623) 2171

This not very well-known cellar is in the Piketberg district, and sells most of its wine to wholesalers. A small quantity is available to the public, and they are happy to sell by mail order and charge the amount to your credit card.

Vin Rouge ♀♀
An everyday Pinotage/Cinsaut blend. Easy-drinking, but of no great distinction. Since when did a plonk drinker look for *distinction* for goodness sake?

Pinotage 🍷🍷
There are some pleasant, earthy aromas and lots of easy, smooth fruit in this fine wine.

Rose 🍷🍷
A pretty pink semi-sweet wine with some cheerful strawberry flavours.

Blanc de Blanc 🍷🍷
An off-dry white wine with a pleasant fruity touch. Very cheap!

Emerald Riesling 🍷
A dry white wine with a low alcohol content.

Late Vintage 🍷🍷
A good, semi-sweet quaffing wine made of Chenin Blanc. Unremarkable.

Premier Grand Crû 🍷
A very dry, tart wine to drink with fish and chips.

Rooi Jerepiko 🍷🍷
A sweet red wine made from Pinotage. Warming for winter evenings.

REBEL WINES

These boxed wines are good value for money and seem to have been selected with care. Alcohol content is a low 10%, so they're ideal for daytime quaffing if you want to stay sober enough to drive home afterwards.

Dry Red 🍷🍷
A very comfortable blended red wine, full of gentle fruitiness. Good drinking value.

Late Harvest 🍷🍷
This wine has some flower scents on the nose and a hint of Hanepoot honey in the mouth. Serve with ice for a pleasant summer drink.

Premier Grand Crû 🍷🍷
A flavour-filled dry white wine that makes an excellent spritzer on a hot day. Goes well with fish too.

Stein ♟♟
A clean semi-sweet white wine with some hints of Hanepoot on the nose. Serve it chilled with curry and rice – a wonderful combination.

Vin de Noir ♟♟
A different name for Blanc de Noir. This pale pink wine is light, fruity, and has a pleasant, fresh nose.

RIEBEEK WINE FARMERS' CO-OP
PO Box 13, Riebeek-Kasteel 6801
Tel: (02244) 213 * Fax: (02244) 281

This rather remote winery is in an attractive setting and has an impressive record of awards and class winners. They are happy to sell wine by mail order and charge it to your credit card.

Pieter Cruythoff Sauvignon Blanc ♟♟
A limited release dry white wine at a very low price. Supply won't last very long.

Colombar ♟♟♟
Lovely wafts of guavas and summer fruit salad make this a most attractive wine. At this price it makes a wonderfully superior house plonk.

Weisser Riesling ♟♟
A delicious off-dry white wine, full of ripe fruit, and a nice clean finish.

Blanc de Noir ♟♟
A pretty, pale-pink wine with rather a pleasant, light fruity character and a touch of sweetness.

Cape Riesling ♟♟
A smooth, easy-drinking dry white wine with some fruity undertones.

Late Harvest ♟♟
A fruity semi-sweet white wine. Serve chilled.

Premier Grand Crû ♟♟♟
A dry white wine with lots of fruit and flavour. Quite full-bodied. Not your everyday acid Grand Crû. This is a treat.

Port ♟♟♟
A very modestly priced little port for casual evenings with friends. Rich and warm, with pleasingly nutty flavours.

RIETRIVIER CO-OP
PO Box 144, Montagu 6720
Tel and Fax: (0234) 41705

Not a very well-known cellar, but this ultimate plonk producer is open to the public and offers some good value wines. They make a large range of 'volkwyne' with incredibly cheerful, bright labels. If you can get them, they're a wonderful conversation piece. They're sold in various sized plastic containers, or 'tapsakke' (R11 for five litres! Beat that!), which are floppy plastic bags with a tap at the bottom.

Colombard ♙♙
A very popular white wine with a pleasant guava nose and clean finish.

Stein ♙♙
This is mostly Colombard, but semi-sweet. Rather a pleasant winter white wine.

Rietrivier Muscadel ♙♙♙
A typical sweet wine with raisins on the nose and in the flavour. Sold with a very elegant silver label.

Rietrivier Vonkelwyn ♙♙
A semi-sweet sparkling wine, attractively packaged and amazingly cheap.

Hanepoot Special ♙
The garishly coloured label tells you immediately, this is a wine for jollers. It's sweet, but not fortified. The alcohol is in fact a rather low 11%.

Sauvignon Blanc ♙♙♙
A certified dry white wine at an incredibly low price. It's worth keeping a couple of cartons on hand for everyday drinking.

Honeybird ♙
A semi-sweet 'people's wine' with an eyeball-searing bright yellow, red and green label. Good entertainment value.

Ladybird ♙♙
A semi-sweet white wine made from Hanepoot. A weekend 'volkwyn' with some rather nice honey flavours and a lowish alcohol content.

Speedy's ♀
The bright blue label shows a little Mexican mouse in a hell of a hurry. This 'people's wine' is made specially for the customers of Speedy's Liquor Store in Oudtshoorn.

ROBERTSON CO-OP
PO Box 37, Robertson 6705
Tel: (02351) 3059 * Fax: (02351) 61415

Plonk drinkers everywhere owe a debt of gratitude to this enterprising co-op for leading the way in the wine packaging revolution. They're challenging the powers that be to allow us all to drink good wine in cheap packaging. All strength to their arms!

Colombard ♀♀♀
A really good plonk for everyday drinking. Keep a case or two on hand for casual quaffing. Gentle and relaxing.

Special Late Harvest ♀♀♀
Made from Gewurztraminer, this mouth-filling wine is packed with the flavour of sun-ripe grapes. A really delicious semi-sweet wine.

Rob Roy Dry Red ♀♀
Unbelievably cheap! Sold in a five-litre box, this is a simple, smooth quaffing wine, with some nice fruity nuances.

Rob Roy Grand Crû ♀♀
A clean, crisp, dry white wine with some quite complex, fruity flavours.

Rob Roy Late Harvest ♀♀
Slightly sweeter than the Stein, this is a juicy and pleasant wine for every day quaffing.

Rob Roy Selected Stein ♀♀
A fruity semi-sweet wine, with some hints of guava on the nose. Try it with bobotie.

Santino Rouge ♀♀
An unusual sweet, red, sparkling wine with lots of lively bubbles. Fun at a party.

Santino Vin Sec ♀♀
A semi-sweet sparkling wine in a very popular style.

Santino Vin Doux ♀
A rather sweet sparkling wine. A bit sticky.

Santino Spumante ♀♀
The muscat in this semi-sweet bubbly makes it really special. Very popular, and you can see why.

500 ml. Tetrapaks ♀♀
These handy little cartons of wine are super for camping, hiking, boating or just enjoying. They're very economical and take up hardly any shelf space. There's a Late Harvest, a Stein, a Dry White and a Dry Red, all reliable, easy-drinking plonks at only R3,00 or so a box. Great value!

ROMANSRIVIER CO-OP
PO Box 108, Wolseley 6830
Tel: (0236) 311070 * Fax: (0236) 311102

This co-op is unusual in that its grapes come from cool mountain vineyards in the Ceres district, although the winery is situated in the usually hot Breede River area. They've improved the quality of their wines steadily, and even won a gold medal in the Veritas competition. Romansrivier was one of the first co-ops to invest in new French oak barrels.

Vino Rood ♀♀
A soft, easy-drinking red plonk made from Pinotage and Cinsaut. Nice price!

Rovino Dry White ♀♀
Sold in a convenient little 500 ml. dumpy bottle, this is a pleasantly crisp wine to drink with a Kentucky fried chicken.

Rovino Red Wine ♀♀
Another handy 500 ml bottled wine. Easy and smooth, this wine slips down without any fuss. Drink it any old time.

Rovino Semi-sweet White ♀♀
Rather a nice, juicy wine. It's sweet, but by no means sticky. In a 500 ml. bottle.

Ceres Colombard ♀♀
This is a delightful dry wine with fresh, fruity undertones.

Ceres Vin Blanc Special Reserve ♟♟
A pleasantly crisp, but fruity semi-sweet white wine for casual drinking.

Blanc de Blanc ♟♟
A beautifully balanced dry white wine with a herbal nose and some fresh fruit salad flavours.

Grand Cru ♟♟
A crisp dry white wine, not as acid as some grand cru wines. Good to serve with grilled yellowtail.

Sweet Hanepoot ♟♟♟
Rich, honey-scented and mouth-filling, this is a good *soetes* for a winter's day.

Port ♟♟
Maybe not one of the greatest ports in the world, but gently sweet and smooth.

ROODEZANDT WINERY
PO Box 164, Robertson 6705
Tel: (02351) 2912 * Fax: (02351) 5074

Roodezandt, right in the main street of Robertson, produces some fine wines, particularly at the sweet end of the range. Most of them can be bought from the winery at about R7,00 a bottle. Great value.

Roodehuiswyn ♟♟
As the name implies, this is a good 'house wine' for everyday enjoyment. Lots of fruit and very drinkable. A plonk drinkers delight.

Red Muscadel ♟♟♟
Delicious honey scents and ripe grape flavours make this a real winner for the *soetes* enthusiasts.

White Muscadel ♟♟♟
I have been told by a winemaker that, if you're blindfolded, you can't tell the difference in flavour between red and white Muscadel. In which case, see above.

Sparkling Wine ♟♟
There are two versions of this everyday bubbly: a semi-sweet and a drier one. Both excellent value and sure to start any party off with a bang.

Colombard 🍷🍷🍷
This wine has been exported to the UK. Lots of guava fruit and nice summer fruit salad flavour. A super-plonk.

Cape Riesling 🍷🍷
A straight-forward dry white wine.

Sauvignon Blanc 🍷🍷
A sound, everyday dry white wine with some clean fruitiness and a crisp finish.

Chardonnay 🍷🍷🍷
Great to find a good Chardonnay (and it really is) at plonk prices. Sun-dried straw on the nose and lots of complex flavours – lemon, caramel, you name it. This is a really serious wine.

Late Harvest 🍷🍷
A pleasant, semi-sweet white wine, juicy and peachy, made from Chenin Blanc.

Special Late Harvest 🍷🍷🍷
A plonk-lover's dream! Lovely scents of summer flowers, and full of soft, sweet fruitiness. Wonderful stuff!

Port 🍷
Quite a respectable little port that will add a classy finish to any meal. A steal at the price!

ROOIBERG CO-OP
PO Box 358, Robertson 6705
Tel: (02351) 3124 * Fax: (02351) 3295

Rooiberg has collected a vast array of awards for their wines. The quality is excellent and they're worth a visit if you're looking for fine wines at bargain prices. They'll rail wines to you and charge your credit card.

Roodewyn 🍷🍷
Amazingly good for the price. It has flavour, body and the potential for a long life. If you have the space, lay down a few cases. It's an investment.

Selected Red Wine 🍷🍷
A lightish, easy-drinking red wine that will go perfectly with a pizza. Good value.

Premier Grand Cru ♟♟
A plain, everyday dry white at a good price.

Selected Stein ♟♟
A good, everyday, late-harvest style wine made from Chenin Blanc and sealed with a screw-cap. Good for casual drinking when there's no special reason for drinking. Who needs a reason?

Selected White ♟♟
A pleasantly crisp dry white wine sold with a screw-cap, which is very practical and saves a few cents.

Rhine Riesling ♟♟
Off-dry, with some fresh, fruity character and a clean finish. A food wine – try it with chicken.

Colombard ♟♟
Off-dry and delicious. You can usually rely on Colombards from Robertson. They invented the stuff here, so they know what to do with it. Good value.

Chenin Blanc ♟♟
An off-dry wine with plenty of flavour. Soft and easy-drinking.

Special Late Harvest ♟♟♟
Great stuff! Full of sweet, warm summer fragrances, like walking through a garden on a hot day.

Blanc de Noir ♟♟♟
Don't let the pretty colour fool you. This off-dry wine has a hefty alcohol level. Great for a party, unless you have to drive home afterwards.

Red Jerepigo ♟♟♟
A real treat for us *soetes* fanatics. It has rich, raisiny flavours with hints of all sorts of other goodies lurking in the complex layers of delight. The ideal wine for sipping in front of a fire on a chilly evening.

Red Muscadel ♟♟♟
Robertson always seems to produce good Muscadels and this is no exception. Rich, raisiny and mouth-filling, but very alcoholic. Delicious.

Port ♟♟♟
One can hardly describe this elegant port as a plonk, but it's within our price limit, so grab it with both hands!

SHOPRITE/CHECKERS

This chain of supermarkets has wisely teamed up with Woodstock wine merchant Oscar Foulkes, and is selling his excellent Eclipse, Mystery and Oscar's Reserve ranges. See under 'Eclipse'.

SIMONDIUM CO-OP
PO Box 19, Simondium 7670
Tel: (02211) 41659 * Fax: (02211) 41402

You'll pass this co-op on the road from Paarl to Franschhoek. It's worth stopping for a tasting. Apart from their normal 750 ml bottles, they sell wine in 500 ml dumpies, two-litre plastic bottles and five-litre boxes.

Pierre Simond Cabernet Sauvignon ♟♟♟
A wonderfully mouth-filling Cabernet, ready to drink, but with some staying power. Not really a plonk at all, but sold at a plonk price. Grab some before they increase the price.

Pierre Simond Ruby Cabernet ♟♟
Lightish and easy-drinking red that could be laid down for future pleasure.

Pierre Simond Special Reserve Red ♟♟♟
This is a Ruby Cabernet that has been given some toasted wood to add flavour and complexity. Quite a serious wine.

Pierre Simond Sauvignon Blanc ♟♟
A very reasonably priced light-bodied dry white wine, with some grassiness on the nose and a pleasant, quite fruity character.

Claret ♟♟
A lightweight red made mostly from Cinsaut and sealed with a sensible screw-cap. Fine for casual summer drinking if served chilled.

Dry Red Special Reserve ♟♟
A medium-bodied dry red with a sweetish nose and some good fruit on the palate.

Grand Crû ♟♟
Sold in a sensible screw-cap bottle, this very dry and slightly acid wine has a hint of grassiness on the nose.

La Festa Dry Red ♟♟
A handy little 500 ml bottle of casual picnic wine. Not great, but easy enough to drink.

La Festa Grand Crû ♟♟
A dry white wine in a 500 ml bottle for everyday easy enjoyment.

La Festa Late Vintage ♟♟
This is quite a juicy little semi-sweet wine in handy 500 ml packs.

Late Vintage ♟♟
A semi-sweet white wine with lots of fruit salad flavours and some honey sweetness that lingers on.

Rosé Sec ♟♟
A pretty, pink wine made clean and dry and sold with a screw-cap. Ideal for summer lunch-time drinking, because you can replace the cap and put it away for tomorrow.

Rosé Semi-sweet ♟♟
This is a pink and pretty wine, with some fresh fruit flavours and juicy sweetness. It has a screw-cap bottle for cheapness and convenience, and should be served chilled.

Stein ♟♟
A soft and fruity semi-sweet wine. Very user-friendly and sold in a screw-cap bottle.

SIMONSIG ESTATE
PO Box 6, Koelenhof 7605
Tel: (021) 8822044 * Fax: (021) 8822545

This family-run estate produces a vast range of wines and is a popular tourist stopping place. They export wines all over the world and are right up front when it comes to marketing. Only one of their wines falls into our plonk range.

Rosé ♟♟♟
This is a very fruity semi-sweet wine with an attractive pink colour and a delicious smooth character. It has a crisp and clean finish and is versatile enough to go with almost any food.

SIMONSVLEI CO-OP
PO Box 584, Suider Paarl 7624
Tel: (02211) 633040 * Fax: (02211) 631240

This very go-ahead cellar was awarded the President's Award for Export Achievement. They deal with thousands of visitors every day during the summer and have wines for all pockets and palates. They also produce a lot of special-label wines for businesses, clubs and restaurants.

Sparkling Wine ♈♈
They make three sparkling wines at Simonsvlei: a dry white, semi-sweet white and a red bubbly. Undemanding and good value for a party or a champagne breakfast.

Blanc de Blanc ♈♈
A pleasantly soft dry white wine with low acidity. Easy to drink. Perfect with deep-fried calamari.

Blanc de Noir ♈♈
This really tasty pale pink wine is off-dry, but drier than most Blanc de Noirs. A fine party plonk, and quite sophisticated.

Humbro ♈♈♈
Made from Hanepoot, this unusual wine is deliciously sweet and full of character. Wonderfully warming on a winter evening.

Late Vintage ♈♈
Another happy wine made from Chenin Blanc with a pretty, flowery nose and lots of fruity flavours. Good value in a screw-cap bottle.

Premier Grand Crû ♈♈
They sell about a million litres of this easy-to-drink, dry white wine made from Chenin Blanc, with a dash of Colombard. Remarkably good value. Available in screw-top bottles or five-litre packs.

Bukettraube ♈♈
Made semi-sweet, this pleasant little wine has some nice blossom scents and a clean finish.

Stein ♈♈
Made from Chenin Blanc, this is a soft, semi-sweet and fruity wine, which is ideal for very relaxed drinking. Good with a Gouda cheese sandwich.

Simonsrood ♗♗♗
This is a light-bodied, blended, dry red wine available in either a corked bottle or one with a screw-cap. Naturally the screw-cap version is the cheapest, so it seems silly to buy the corked one. Very smooth and fruity, this really fine plonk is also available in five-litre boxes for inexpensive drinking.

Stein ♗♗
You can buy this fruity semi-sweet wine in two versions: the screw-cap bottle or the five-litre box. It's a fun wine, which is fresh and juicy.

Non-vintage Port ♗♗
They also make a vintage port at Simonsvlei, but this is the cheap one. Not bad for winter sipping, or drinking by the camp-fire at night.

SLANGHOEK CO-OP
PO Box 75, Rawsonville 6845
Tel: (0231) 91130 * Fax: (0231) 91891

Known for its sweet dessert wines, this co-op near Rawsonville is now producing a whole range of fine table wines at very reasonable prices.

Pinotage ♗♗♗
A splendid dry red wine with a touch of wood, some very pleasant fruitiness and a nice tannic grip. At R10 a bottle, it's almost beyond the plonker's pocket, but is a great little wine.

Cabernet Sauvignon ♗♗
A nice nutty, fruity red wine. Could be laid down.

Chenin Blanc ♗♗
A very flavour-packed dry white wine. At this price, an ideal house-wine.

Riesling/Semillon ♗♗
A pleasing dry white wine with lots of character.

Chardonnay/Sauvignon Blanc ♗♗
We're getting into serous stuff here! A mouth-filling dry white with some lively fruit flavours. Almost too elegant to be called a plonk, but we plonkers are easily capable of adapting to good wine.

Special Late Harvest ♛♛
Good, juicy semi-sweet wine with a nice balance. You could drink this with Chinese take-aways.

Vonkelwyn ♛♛
Nice to have a cheerful little sweet bubbly at a plonk price. Just fine for a casual party.

Soet Hanepoot ♛♛♛
Liquid gold! South African should concentrate on exporting these superb sweet wines. Or better still, let's drink them all ourselves.

SOETWYNBOERE CO-OP

This Montagu Co-op has changed it's name to Cogman's Co-op. Their wines are listed under the new name.

SPAR WINES

Available in five-litre boxes from Spar supermarkets.

Carnival Dry Red ♛♛
A light-bodied, fruity red wine.

Carnival Grand Crû ♛♛♛
An unusually flavourful wine for a Grand Cru – crisp, but fruity and fresh.

Carnival Late Harvest ♛♛
Sweetish white wine. A bit sticky, but drinkable.

Carnival Stein ♛♛
A juicy semi-sweet white wine. Not very memorable, but fine for drinking with smoked snoek.

SPRUITDRIFT CO-OP
PO Box 129, Vredendal 8160
Tel: (0271) 33086 * Fax: (0271) 32937

This is a good cellar to visit during early spring, when the West Coast's wild flowers are in bloom. Some excellent value for money wines can be bought from this co-op.

Blanc de Noir ♟♟♟
This one is a deeper colour than most Blanc de Noirs. Delicious flavours and wonderful honey hints. A rather special, off-dry drink.

Premier Grand Cru ♟♟
Available in either corked bottles or with screw, caps at 50 cents a bottle less. Fresh and crisp.

Cabernet Sauvignon ♟♟
A modestly priced Cabernet which is medium, bodied and nicely balanced for easy drinking.

Pinotage ♟♟
Previously sold as 'Dry Red', this is a relaxed, easy-drinking red with some nice fruit. A braai wine.

Late Harvest ♟♟
This is a light, juicy semi-sweet white wine that's won plenty of awards. It is available in a corked bottle, or in one with a screw cap at a slightly lower price. By all means pay the higher price if you go for corks.

Red Muscadel ♟♟
For those who enjoy a warming glass of *soetes* this is a winner. Very raisiny and fruity and good value.

Riesling ♟♟
A clean, dry white wine with some fruit in the background. It could be pleasant with a fish braai.

SWARTLAND CO-OP
PO Box 95, Malmesbury 7300
Tel: (0224) 21134 * Fax: (0224) 21750

This giant, flourishing co-op, with 90 members, is unusual in that they market all their own wines, rather than selling the bulk of it to wholesalers. They compete with the country's best and they often win. They have featured so often in Wine-of-the-Month Club selections that members are starting to complain about favouritism! There's a wide range of five-litre and two-litre Swartland boxes at prices that make drinking really affordable.

Blanc de Noir ♉♉♉
An attractive, pale coral coloured wine with juicy berry flavours, but not too sweet. Deliciously crisp.

Cinsaut ♉♉
A dry red wine that's uncomplicated and easy to drink. An enthusiast could call this the Tassies of the Swartland.

Dry Red ♉♉
The house blend, made of Pinotage and sold in various packages, including boxes. Good, reliable and relaxing.

Grand Crû ♉♉
A no-nonsense dry white wine. Plain and simple, without any pretensions.

Late Vintage ♉♉
A nice, juicy semi-sweet wine. Not much character, but sound.

Pinotage ♉♉
A nicely understated red wine that goes well with food. It is pleasant, easy drinking and not pushy.

Red Jerepiko ♉♉
A raisiny sweet wine with lots of sunny West Coast character. Warming and generous.

White Jerepiko ♉♉♉
Very sweet and full-bodied, rich and warm. A rock angler's first aid kit in a bottle.

Rosé ♉♉
A pretty pink wine, blended from a red and a white wine, semi-sweet, very juicy and fruity, with a touch of acidity for freshness.

Stein ♀♀
A semi-sweet white wine that's very smooth and easy to drink. Available in bottles or boxes.

Tinta Barocca ♀♀♀
A delightful dry red with loads of flavour, and quite a lot of alcohol too. A good braai wine.

Vin de Noir ♀♀♀
One of the nicest Blanc de Noirs around. Fruity but very fresh and crisp, with a clean finish. Impressive. In two and five-litre boxes. Amazing value.

Fernao Pires ♀♀
An off-dry white wine with an interesting spicy nose. Quiet and undemanding. Good value.

Sparkling Wine ♀♀
They produce four different sparkling wines at Swartland, all at around R9 a bottle. There's a dry Cuvee Brut, a semi-sweet Demi-Sec, a sweet Vin Doux and a semi-sweet red one called Rosette. All plain, fun bubblies for any celebration.

TASSENBERG ♀♀♀
Undoubtedly South Africa's favourite plonk, it is the wine that started millions of students on the slippery slope to wine enjoyment. SFW sells about 500,000 bottles of this excellent red wine every year, and the price has been kept down, in the region of an incredible five rands a bottle. It's available in corked bottles for those who want to lay it down, and it does mature very well. It also comes in five-litre boxes. The benchmark plonk!

TAVERNA ROUGE ♀♀♀
Probably the most serious rival to Tassies, this fine red plonk is produced by Distillers Corporation and is available from bottle stores everywhere. Some plonk drinkers claim it's better than Tassies, but it can't match the sales. It retails at about the same price as Tassies, and is a smooth, easy-to-drink wine with no pretensions (except that it has been given some wood maturation, which is rather up-market). It's good value and goes well with Italian food.

TOCORNAL CABERNET SAUVIGNON 🍷🍷🍷
The first imported plonk to get into the SA Plonk Buyer's Guide! This amazingly good Chilean red wine is one of the fruitiest red wines around, packed with ripe black current juiciness and backed up by soft tannin and a touch of easy acidity. You could drink this all day. And it's sold for less than R10 a bottle! Incredible value! Available at Checkers/Shoprite, Macro and Wine Warehouse in Woodstock.

TRAWAL WYNKELDERS
PO Box 2, Klawer 8154
Tel and Fax: (02724) 61616

This west coast co-op is a friendly place to visit. It produces a modest range of wines made from the grapes of about 50 farmers. They're geared for mail order and prices are incredibly low.

Blanc de Blanc 🍷🍷🍷
A pleasant dry white wine, with crisp fruit salad flavours and quite a lively acid bite to it. Drink this with a West Coast kreef.

Hárslevelü 🍷🍷
A dryish white wine. Not a great deal of character, but uncomplicated and reliable.

Late Harvest 🍷🍷
Semi-sweet white wine with lush hints of muscat honey on the nose and palate.

Muscat D'Or 🍷🍷🍷
A very juicy, ripe-grape sort of wine, made from good old Hanepoot. Semi-sweet and smooth. Definitely a superior plonk.

Premier Grand Crû 🍷🍷
A blended dry white wine with lots of character. It should have, as it contains about four different grape varieties.

Travino Spumante 🍷🍷
A semi-sweet bubbly with quite a low alcohol content. Not great, but fine for a teenage party. With orange juice it's pretty harmless and it makes them feel grown-up.

TULBAGH CO-OP
PO Box 85, Tulbagh 6820
Tel: (0236) 301001 * Fax. (0236) 301358

This is one of the few co-operative cellars that market all their own wines. There are some bargains to be had here and the wines are being exported to several countries. Some of the wines are now available in cheap, but quite attractive, plastic bottles, as well as five-litre boxes.

Blanc de Noir ▼▼
A slightly sweet, pale-pink wine made from Pinotage and given a few tiny bubbles for zest. A breakfast wine.

Claret ▼▼
Quite a gutsy, full-bodied red wine made of Pinotage, Cinsaut and Tinta Barocca. Simple and easy-drinking.

Grand Cru ▼▼▼
Lots of interesting flavour in this dry white wine. Really good plonk.

Fernao Pirez ▼
Spicy on the nose, but flattish flavours.

Bukettraube ▼▼
A nice delicate semi-sweet white wine with some flowery scents and gentle fruit.

Late Harvest ▼▼
Semi-sweet and packed with fresh fruit taste.

Ruby Cabernet ▼▼
A smooth, fruity red wine with a sweetish aftertaste. Some hints of wood too. Good value.

Pinotage ▼▼
A light-bodied red wine to drink lightly chilled in summer.

Jerepigo ▼▼▼
A sweet red wine with a complex blend of flavours. A warming winter drink, or a delightful foil to a hot curry.

Port ▼▼
Well, a sweet red wine, really. Not like other ports, but rather pleasant and fruity.

VAALHARTS CO-OP
PO Box 4, Hartswater 8570
Tel: (05332) 425111 * Fax: (05332) 42682

This rather remote cellar is the most northerly winery in South Africa.

Overvaal Dry Red ♟♟
A light, dry red for summer drinking, served cool.

Overvaal Sparkling Doux ♟♟
This is really a wine for a teenage party. Sweet, pink and cool drinky with a lively bubble. Fun, and it goes with birthday cake.

Overvaal Jerepigo ♟♟♟
As can be expected in this sun-drenched area, this is a wine full of warmth and sunny sweetness. It's smooth and remarkably elegant. A super-*soetes*.

VALLEY WINES

Produced by Gilbeys, these are reliable, down-market wines for everyday drinking. Interestingly, they often score well in blind tastings. Available in five-litre boxes and two-litre jugs.

Smooth Red ♟♟♟
A medium-bodied red wine with a bit of bite to it. I think you could lay this one down if you really wanted to. It's a super braai or pasta wine.

Premier Grand Crû ♟♟
Very dry white wine with a nice touch of acidity. Good for hot days. Serve well chilled or even with ice.

Selected Stein ♟♟
Semi-sweet, tasty and fruity. A nice summer drink, served really cold.

Semi-Sweet Rosé ♟♟
An easy-drinking wine for casual quaffing. It has a nice clean character and a very pretty colour. Good value.

VAN LOVEREN
PO Box 19, Klaasvoogds 6707
Tel: (0234) 51505 * Fax: (0234) 51336

Most of the Van Loveren wines are rather too grand for inclusion in a book of plonk, but two Blancs de Noir fall well within our range.

Blanc de Noir Shiraz ♛♛♛
A wine with a very pale coral pink colour, soft flavours and berry-fruit juiciness on the palate. The finish has just a touch of tannic bite to add character. A very unusual wine.

Blanc de Noir Red Muscadel ♛♛♛
A pale, almost cream coloured wine made semi-sweet, with the honey scents typical of a muscat grape. An ideal day-time drink. with lowish alcohol

---

VAT OHIO

Boxed wines made by the Rooiberg Co-op in the Robertson area.

Grand Crû ♛♛
A rather ordinary dry white wine for casual boozing.

Late Harvest ♛♛
Semi-sweet and quite drinkable, if unspectacular.

Stein Select ♛♛
Fruity, semi-sweet and quite gentle. Easy to sip when served well chilled.

VAUGHAN JOHNSON WINES
V&A Waterfront, Cape Town 8000
Tel: (021) 4192121 * Fax: (021) 4190040

In his attractive wine shop at the V&A Waterfront, Vaughan Johnson is putting a lot of the fun back into wine. In a bold move, Johnson is clashing head-on with the law in a bid to have wine shops open on Sundays. We hope he succeeds. Johnson understands plonk drinkers and is probably the first wine merchant actually to label his plonk as 'Plonk'. That's honesty for you!

Good Everyday Red ♛♛
Wonderfully drinkable and soft, with quite a complex, layered character. From the Swartland.

Good Everyday Dry White ♟♟
Well, the label says it all. Just drink it.

Seriously Good Plonk (white) ♟♟
Again, what more can we add? It really is. And it comes in a litre bottle for added value.

Seriously Good Plonk (red) ♟♟
Another litre bottle of pleasure from the Stellenbosch area, made of Pinotage and Cinsaut. Soft and very drinkable.

As You Like it (white) ♟♟
Made from Chenin Blanc, it's a dry white wine from Franschhoek. Some nice fruit salad flavours in here.

As You Like It (red) ♟♟
A blended red from Stellenbosch, quite full-bodied and smooth. Good value.

Waterfront Captain's Claret ♟♟
What yachtsman could resist having a few bottles of this one on board? It's a light-bodied red wine made from Tinta Barocca, fruity and fresh, and rather pleasant served chilled.

Really Good White ♟♟
A softish dry white wine with subtle Sauvignon Blanc character understated but definitely there. You'd expect it to cost a lot more than it does. There's a Really Good Red too, but it's a bit costly for us plonk drinkers.

VERGENOEGD ESTATE
PO Box 1, Faure 7131
Tel: (024) 43248

This low-profile estate on the Swartklip-Stellenbosch road is well worth a visit. It's a very attractive old farmstead surrounded by ducks and geese. It's not a member of the wine route, but the red wines have a steady and loyal following.

Cinsaut ♟♟♟
A really good, honest red wine with lots of flavour and fruit. Soft and subtle for casual drinking. Amazing value.

VILLIERSDORP CO-OP
PO Box 14, Villiersdorp 7170
Tel: (0225) 31120 * Fax: (0225) 31833

This cellar uses grapes from a wide range of areas, so they are able to make some interesting wines. Prices are low and quality is not bad at all. There's also a pleasant coffee shop to visit while you're considering your wine purchases.

Blanc de Noir
A rather pretty peach colour, this wine is made from Pinotage, semi-sweet and pleasantly smooth. There's loads of juicy fruitiness for relaxed drinking.

Grand Crû
A very dry white wine with some melon flavour. Not as dull as many other Premier Grand Cru's. It has quite a pleasing fruitiness, with a nice crisp finish.

Late Vintage
A semi-sweet white wine with a hint of sun-warmed straw on the nose. Not very much character, but quite drinkable.

Perlé
A light, off-dry sparkling wine. Good for a party and cheap enough to drink in quite large quantities! Try it mixed with orange juice.

Pinotage
This is a bargain! A red plonk that's been given some wood maturation to add glamour and complexity. Made for early drinking, and very soft. Good value.

Kroonland Chardonnay
Amazingly good value for a Chardonnay. Young and fresh flavoured, with clean lemon-lime flavours. An impressive plonk.

Semillon
Watch this wine. Semillon is one of the varietals of the future. Plonk drinkers should grab this chance to sample it at a reasonable price. An unusual dry white wine you could actually keep for a year or two.

Riesling
Here's a really elegant plonk, full of interesting fruit, but light and easy-drinking.

Hanepoot Jerepiko ♀♀
Who could resist a gently sweet wine like this? Full of ripe grape flavours, honey and nuts. A *soetes* drinker's dream.

Port ♀♀
A lightish port, made from Tinta Barocca. You could drink this one chilled, to cheer up a gloomy winter's day.

VINO ROMA BIANCO ♀
Once called Roma White, this is a dry, rather astringent white wine, but with a loyal following. OK if you like lots of acid.

VIRGINIA ♀
It's always been a mystery to me why they advertise Virginia as a 'wine for men who enjoy being men'. It's not a particularly alcoholic wine, or rough and tough. Just a rather simple semi-sweet white wine. The producers claim it's the biggest selling wine in South Africa, so the advertising must have worked. Amazing!

VLOTTENBURG CO-OP
PO Box 40, Vlottenburg 7604
Tel: (021) 8813828 * Fax: (021) 8813357

Vlottenberg, just outside Stellenbosch, is an easy winery for Capetonians to visit. There are some excellent bargains to be found at this little cellar. While you're there, try some of their grander wines too.

Blanc de Blanc ♀♀♀
Sold in a litre bottle, this clean dry white wine slips down easily and has a nice acid crispness. Excellent value.

Sauvignon Blanc ♀♀
This very refreshing white wine has some fruity blackcurrent flavours and a clean finish. Worth keeping for a year or two.

Chenin Blanc ♈♈
An off-dry white wine that's easy to drink. Unspectacular, but tasty.

Gewurztraminer ♈♈♈
A delightfully scented wine with lots of fruity flavour, semi-sweet, but beautifully crisp and clean. Exactly right for a mutton curry.

Special Late Harvest ♈♈
Semi-sweet and very drinkable. Great for casual evenings talking rubbish with a few pals.

Rouge ♈♈
Good value in a litre bottle. A robust, plummy, everyday red plonk with a bit of a tannic bite.

Reserve ♈♈♈
This is a really classy wine, made mainly from Shiraz and given some oak maturation. Plonk fans can raise their screw-caps in salute to a fine wine.

VREDENDAL CO-OP
PO Box 75, Vredendal 8160
Tel: (0271) 31080 * Fax: (0271) 33476

If you're looking for unusual wine labels, try some of these innovative designs. This is one of the biggest co-ops in the country, and manager Giel Swiegers enjoys using West Coast and African names on his labels. You'll find several of these in the top United Kingdom liquor stores, sold under brand names like Namaqua.

Grand Cru ♈♈♈
Not your usual arid Grand Cru, this one is very dry, but full of wonderful fruit flavour at a very friendly price. An elegant food wine.

Blanc de Noir ♈♈
An off-dry, pale pink wine, made from Pinotage. A juicy mouthful of ripe berries. Very easy to drink.

Fernao Pires ♈♈♈
This semi-sweet white wine has a delicate, honey aroma and a pleasing touch of sweetness. Excellent value.

Spesiale Laatoes ♈♈
A rich, mouth-filling semi-sweet white wine, with lots of fruity sweetness and a clean finish.

Goiya Kgeisje ♀♀♀
Giel says this name comes from the old Bushman expression meaning 'first wine'. How the Bushmen knew about wine, I have no idea, but why ruin a good story? Usually the first wine in the country to be certified each season. Clean, fruity and crisp. Very tasty and the Bushman painting labels are collectors' items.

Bukettraube ♀♀
A light, fruity semi-sweet wine, quite low in alcohol and very reasonably priced.

Meisje ♀♀
An off-dry white wine, light-hearted and low in alcohol. Fresh and lively. Perfect for an outdoor summer lunch.

Dry Red ♀♀
A plainish, everyday red. Inexpensive and unspectacular, but quite drinkable. The ideal drink for an afternoon of rugby on TV.

VREDENHEIM ESTATE WINES
PO Box 369, Stellenbosch 7599
Tel: (021) 8813637 * Fax: (021) 8813296

One of the few Cape wine cellars with a female winemaker. A feature of these wines is their unusual and bright labels. Vredenheim, next door to Vlottenburg co-op, is well worth a visit.

Dry Red ♀♀♀
A fruity blended red wine with a nice subtle tannic bite, for everyday enjoyment. Great with steak.

WABOOMSRIVIER CO-OP
PO Box 24, Breërivier 6858
Tel: (02324) 730 * Fax: (02324) 731

Most of the wine from this interesting cellar goes to the big wholesalers, but there are often good bargains to be found here. They accept a minimum order of 12 bottles and will rail wines to you.

Grand Cru ♀♀
A dry white wine made from Colombard, with plenty of pleasant fruit. Very drinkable. Also available in five-litre packs, making it good value.

Riesling 🍷🍷
Dry and clean. Not remarkable, but enjoyable for everyday drinking.

Chenin Blanc Late Harvest 🍷🍷
A semi-sweet wine with some pleasing floral scents. Very low price, particularly if you buy the five-litre pack.

Chenin Blanc Late Harvest 🍷🍷
A nice, fruity semi-sweet wine with a mouth-filling character. Good value.

Perlé Sparkling Wine 🍷🍷
If you want to buy bubbly for a party, you can't do much better than this price! It's a really budget-priced, semi-sweet sparkling wine that's light and pretty.

Pinotage 🍷🍷
A pleasant and easy-drinking red plonk, with some light woodiness and lots of fruit.

Rubellite 🍷🍷
A semi-sweet sparkling rosé wine, that's soft and fruity and quite lively. A breakfast wine.

Ruby Cabernet 🍷🍷🍷
A reasonably priced red plonk with some sweetish berry aromas and lots of pleasant fruit on the palate. Easy drinking and good value.

Hanepoot Jeripigo 🍷🍷🍷
Modestly priced for a fortified wine. Deliciously smooth and honey sweet. A lovely *soetes*.

Port 🍷🍷
Not a bad little port, this! It even has that dusty character you get with really old ports and is not stickily sweet, like some of the cheap ports. Try it.

WAMAKERSVALLEI CO-OP
PO Box 509, Wellington 7657
Tel: (02211) 31582 Fax (02211) 33194

This co-op specialises in light, easy-drinking wines with quite low alcohol contents. But don't be fooled by the light touch – some classy award winners have come out of Wamakersvallei in recent years.

Cinsaut ♀♀
A smooth, unpretentious and nicely rounded dry red wine for everyday drinking.

Pinotage ♀♀♀
A light-bodied, easy-drinking dry red wine with gentle fruity flavours. A delicious summer red.

Laatoes ♀♀
Fruity and sweet, this white wine is made from Chenin Blanc. Good with curry.

Premier Grand Crû ♀♀
Fresh and grassy, this is a crisp, light white wine that's very dry, but interesting.

Stein ♀♀
Made from Chenin Blanc grapes, with a nice round sweetness. It's a good fruity wine at a low price.

Bon Ami wines ♀♀
These handy 500 ml dumpy bottles are good for everyday drinking at a low price. There's a dry white, an off-dry white and a light-bodied red. Great picnic fare.

WELLINGTON CO-OP
PO Box 520, Wellington 7657
Tel: (02211) 31163 * Fax: (02211) 32423

This cellar is a plonk lover's dream! Every wine on the latest price list fell well within our R10 limit, even the Cabernet Sauvignon! Some great finds here. They're certainly not cheap-and-nasty, either! The co-op has gathered several awards at wine shows.

Cabernet Sauvignon ♀♀
You could lay this one down and end up with a really good wine. Come to think of it, drink it now. It's good stuff.

Merlot ♟♟♟
A nice herbal nose and lots of fruity flavours in this mouth-filling red wine. A good drink at a good price!

Pinotage ♟♟♟
This is a very pleasant, soft and juicy red wine, with lots of fruit on the palate and a nice clean finish. You can see why Pinotage is gaining in popularity. (But it took the British wine buyers to wake us up to its potential.)

Grand Crû ♟♟
A nice, smooth, elegant, but dry wine with a slightly grassy character, blended from Sauvignon Blanc and Chenin Blanc. Excellent value.

Stein ♟♟
Here's a sweetish, fruity white wine for easy, casual quaffing on its own or with food. Very good value.

Special Late Vintage ♟♟♟
Incredible value! This delicious semi-sweet wine is packed with fruit and honey flavours. A summer's day in a bottle. You can't go wrong buying a case of this. Two cases!

Late Vintage ♟♟
Less spectacular than the Special Late Vintage, but fruity and juicy.

Hanepoot Jerepigo ♟♟♟
A sweet, warming wine full of rich raisin flavours. Nicely balanced and not sticky.

Port ♟♟
Not a great or classical port. Maybe it should be laid down for a few years to soften a bit.

WELMOED CO-OP
PO Box 465, Stellenbosch 7599
Tel: (021) 8813800 * Fax: (021) 8813434

An attractive and easily accessible winery where you can get a good lunch and browse in the self-service wine shop. Like many Cape wineries, Welmoed is exporting a good deal of its production. A nice place to visit.

Blanc de Noir ♛♛♛
An off-dry wine with a pretty coral pink colour and some fresh strawberry scents and flavours. A lively summer drink to be enjoyed well chilled.

Red Jerepigo ♛♛
Rich and sweet wine, with some very hearty raisin flavour and sunny warmth.

Rouge Royale ♛♛
A very quaffable, everyday red wine made from Pinotage and Shiraz with a touch of wood. A smooth, fruity wine for casual drinking.

Special Late Harvest ♛♛
A full-bodied, semi-sweet white wine.

Late Vintage ♛♛
A nicely balanced semi-sweet white wine. Ordinary, but a serviceable plonk.

Chenin Blanc ♛♛
Made off-dry, this is a soft, easy-drinking wine to enjoy with spare ribs or pork chops.

WESTERN PROVINCE CELLARS
This chain of liquor stores has its own brand name, Monterey (see Monterey Wines).

WINDMEUL CO-OP
PO Box 2013, Windmeul 7630
Tel: (02211) 638043 * Fax: (02211) 638614

Tucked away at the back of the Paarl mountain, this rather low-key cellar produces some good value, award-winning wines, particularly the reds. They sell from the cellar only, so you won't find them in your local liquor store, or be able to order them by mail.

Moulin Rouge ♟♟♟
An excellent blend of Cabernet and Merlot, unwooded and full of delicious fruitiness. A nice little bite of tannin leaves your palate clean.

Paarl Cinsaut ♟♟♟
If you're looking for a red house wine for everyday drinking, this could be it. Soft and fruity, with lots of complex flavours unfolding as you sip. A rather special plonk.

Paarl Pinotage ♟♟♟
Very juicy and fruity. Quite a complex red that will go down well with Italian foods or the Sunday braai. Or just drink it on its own. It's very good.

Chenin Blanc ♟♟
A big, mouth-filling dry white wine with lots of summer fruitiness on the nose and palate.

Paarl Riesling ♟♟
A dry white wine with a hint of crisp fruit.

Sauvignon Blanc ♟♟
Very dry and crisp, with some typical grassy, Sauvignon Blanc character.

Bukettraube ♟♟
A fragrant white wine, more off-dry than semi-sweet. Soft and easy drinking at a modest price.

WITZENBERG WINES

These are budget-priced wines, made by the Cape Wine and Brandy Co in Stellenbosch, for everyday drinking.

Perlé ♙♙
A semi-sweet white wine that's actually remarkable value for money. It's made pleasantly fruity with plenty of fresh grape flavour and aroma coming through and an interesting little prickle of tiny bubbles for excitement. It has enough flavour to make it suitable for drinking with boboties and mild curries.

Roodekeur ♙
A red wine. There are better ones on the market.

Stein Select ♙♙
A rather plain, semi-sweet white wine.

WOOLWORTHS WINES

Woolworths wine-buying team manage to round up some pretty spectacular wines to fit all palates and pockets. Probably the best for plonk lovers are the ones sold in the one-litre and and 250 ml tetrapaks. They're nicely portable and not at all bad-drinking. Ideal boat wines, as they pack into small spaces and don't roll about.

Petit Vin Dry Red ♙♙
A light and fresh dry red wine with some fruit.

Petit Vin Dry White ♙♙
Made from Chenin Blanc, although our strange wine laws make it illegal to say so on the box. Clean and refreshing. A summer wine.

Petit Vin Late Harvest ♙♙
A pleasantly juicy semi-sweet wine for relaxed enjoyment.

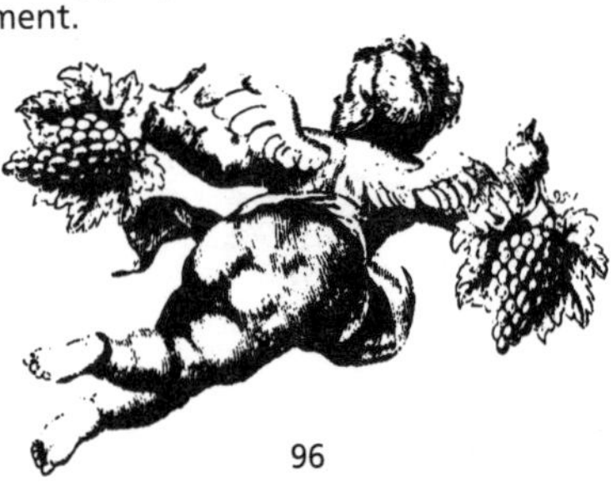